# Message from Richard Cordray

## Director of the CFPB

At the Consumer Financial Protection Bureau, we are the nation's first federal agency whose sole focus is protecting consumers in the financial marketplace. Financial products like mortgages, credit cards, and student loans involve some of the most important financial transactions in people's lives. In the Dodd-Frank Act, Congress created the Bureau to stand on the side of consumers and ensure they are treated fairly in the financial marketplace. Since we opened our doors, we have been focused on making consumer financial markets work better for the American people, and helping them improve their financial lives.

In this, our sixth Semi-Annual Report to Congress and the President, we describe the Bureau's efforts to achieve this vital mission. Through fair rules, consistent oversight, appropriate enforcement of the law, and broad-based consumer engagement, the Bureau is helping to restore American families' trust in consumer financial markets, protect consumers from improper conduct, and ensure access to fair, competitive, and transparent markets.

During this reporting period, we have helped secure orders through enforcement actions for more than $1.6 billion in relief for consumers who fell victim to various violations of consumer financial protection laws. We brought numerous enforcement actions for various violations of the Dodd-Frank Act, including one against Bank of America related to credit card add-on products which provided approximately $727 million in relief to harmed consumers. The Bureau also obtained approximately $92 million in debt relief from Colfax Capital Corporation and Culver Capital, LLC for harm to about 17,000 U.S. servicemembers and other consumers involving the company's predatory lending scheme, and also filed suit against Frederick J. Hanna & Associates for operating a debt collection lawsuit mill in which the company filed more than 350,000 lawsuits in Georgia alone between 2009 and 2013.

The Bureau also issued a number of proposed or final rules. In April 2014, we proposed revisions to the remittance rule to clarify some of the rule's new consumer protections while providing federally insured institutions with additional time to provide more accurate disclosures in certain cases. The Bureau issued a final rule in connection with this proposal in August 2014. In May 2014, we proposed a rule to promote more effective annual privacy disclosures from financial institutions to their customers. The proposal would allow companies that limit their disclosure of customers' nonpublic personal information and meet other requirements to satisfy their annual notice requirement by posting the notices online in more circumstances and delivering them individually in fewer circumstances. In August 2014, the Bureau published a proposed rule in the *Federal Register* to improve information reported about the residential mortgage market, which would shed more light on consumers' access to mortgage credit by updating the reporting requirements for the Home Mortgage Disclosure Act and simplify the reporting process for financial institutions.

To promote informed financial decision making, we have continued to develop useful tools for consumers, including the *Your Money, Your Goals* toolkit, a comprehensive guide to empowered financial decision-making that covers topics like budgeting daily expenses, managing debt, and avoiding financial tricks and traps. We also published a report to promote financial wellness in the workplace, which contains case studies designed to educate employers about practices that can improve employees' financial health and increase worker productivity.

The premise that lies at the very heart of our mission is that consumers deserve to be treated fairly in the financial marketplace and to have someone stand on their side when that does not happen. To this end, since launching Consumer Response operations on July 21, 2011 through September 30, 2014, the CFPB has handled approximately 460,700 consumer complaints, including complaints on credit reporting, debt collection, money transfers, bank accounts and services, credit cards, mortgages, vehicle loans, payday loans, student loans, and certain other consumer financial products or services, including prepaid cards, debt settlement services, credit repair services, and pawn and title loans.

The progress we have made has been possible thanks to the engagement of hundreds of thousands of Americans who have utilized our consumer education tools, submitted complaints, participated in rulemakings, and told us their stories through our website and at numerous public meetings from coast to coast. We have benefited as well from an ongoing dialogue and constructive engagement with the institutions we supervise, with community banks and credit unions with whom we regularly meet, as well as with consumer advocates throughout the country. Our progress has also resulted from the extraordinary work of the Bureau's employees—dedicated public servants who are committed to promoting a healthy consumer financial marketplace. Each day, we work to accomplish the goals of renewing people's trust in the marketplace and ensuring that markets for consumer financial products and services are fair, transparent, and competitive. These goals not only support consumers in all financial circumstances, but also help responsible businesses compete on a level playing field, and reinforce the stability of our economy as a whole.

In the years to come, we look forward to continuing to fulfill Congress's vision of an agency dedicated to cultivating a consumer financial marketplace based on transparency, responsible practices, sound innovation, and excellent customer service.

Sincerely,

Richard Cordray
Director

# Table of contents

# 1. Executive summary

The Consumer Financial Protection Bureau (CFPB or Bureau) presents this Semi-Annual Report to the President, Congress, and the American people, in fulfillment of its statutory responsibility and commitment to accountability and transparency. This report provides an update on the Bureau's mission, activities, accomplishments, and publications since the last Semi-Annual Report, and provides additional information required by the Dodd-Frank Wall Street Reform and Consumer Protection Act (Dodd-Frank or Dodd-Frank Act).[1]

The Dodd-Frank Act created the Bureau as the nation's first federal agency with a mission of focusing solely on consumer financial protection and making consumer financial markets work for American consumers, responsible businesses, and the economy as a whole. In the wake of the financial crisis of 2008-2010, the President and Congress recognized the need to address widespread failures in consumer protection and the rapid growth in irresponsible lending practices that preceded the crisis. To remedy these failures, the Dodd-Frank Act consolidated most Federal consumer financial protection authority in the Bureau.[2] The Dodd-Frank Act charged the Bureau with, among other things:

---

[1] Appendix B provides a guide to the Bureau's response to the reporting requirements of Section 1016(c) of the Dodd-Frank Act. The last Semi-Annual Report was published in May 2014 and may be viewed at: http://files.consumerfinance.gov/f/201405_cfpb_semi-annual-report.pdf.

[2] Previously, seven different federal agencies were responsible for rulemaking, supervision, and enforcement relating to consumer financial protection. The agencies which previously administered statutes transferred to the Bureau are the Federal Reserve Board (and the Federal Reserve Banks) (Board or FRB), Department of Housing and Urban Development (HUD), Federal Deposit Insurance Corporation (FDIC), Federal Trade Commission (FTC), National Credit Union Administration (NCUA), Office of the Comptroller of the Currency (OCC), and Office of Thrift Supervision .

- Ensuring that consumers have timely and understandable information to make responsible decisions about financial transactions;

- Protecting consumers from unfair, deceptive, or abusive acts and practices, and from discrimination;

- Monitoring compliance with Federal consumer financial law and taking appropriate enforcement action to address violations;

- Identifying and addressing outdated, unnecessary or unduly burdensome regulations;

- Enforcing Federal consumer financial law consistently in order to promote fair competition;

- Ensuring that markets for consumer financial products and services operate transparently and efficiently to facilitate access and innovation; and

- Conducting financial education programs.[3]

The Bureau has continued its efforts to listen and respond to consumers and industry, to be a resource for the American consumer, and to develop into a great institution worthy of the responsibility conferred on it by Congress.

# 1.1   Listening to consumers

Listening and responding to consumers is central to the Bureau's mission. The Bureau continues to provide consumers with numerous ways to make their voices heard. Consumers nationwide have engaged with the Bureau through public field hearings, listening events, roundtables, and town halls, and through our website, consumerfinance.gov. Consumer engagement strengthens the Bureau's understanding of current issues in the ever-changing consumer financial marketplace and informs every aspect of the Bureau's work, including research, rule writing, supervision, and enforcement.

---

[3] *See* Dodd-Frank Act, Pub. L. No. 111-203, Sec. 1021 (b) and (c).

The Bureau has continued to improve and expand the capabilities of its Office of Consumer Response (Consumer Response) to receive, process, and facilitate responses to consumer complaints. For example, in July 2014, the Bureau added complaints about prepaid cards to the already wide range of products and services for which it accepts complaints, and from October 1, 2013 through September 30, 2014, has received about 400 complaints on this topic. Consumer Response has also continued to develop and update a robust public Consumer Complaint Database. The database updates nightly and is populated by over 294,400 complaints from consumers about financial products and services from all over the country. In July 2014, the Bureau proposed a policy to give consumers the option to share the stories behind their complaints in the database, and received over 130 unique comments from the public and industry. Over the coming months, the Bureau will continue its evaluation of these comments and the potential expansion of the database to include consumers' complaint narratives.

## 1.2 Delivering for American consumers and leveling the playing field

The Bureau has continued to expand its efforts to serve and protect consumers in the financial marketplace. The Bureau seeks to serve as a resource on the macro level, by writing clear rules of the road and enforcing consumer financial laws in ways that improve the consumer financial marketplace, and on the micro level, by helping individual consumers resolve their specific issues with financial products and services. While the various divisions of the Bureau play different roles in carrying out the Bureau's mission, they all work together to protect and educate consumers, help level the playing field for participants, and fulfill the Bureau's statutory obligations and mission under the Dodd-Frank Act. In all of its work, the Bureau strives to act in ways that are fair, reasonable, and transparent.

We are working to provide tools and information to develop practical skills and support sound financial decision making directly to consumers. These skills include being able to ask questions and to plan ahead. One way we are doing this is with our online tool, Ask CFPB. This tool provides answers to over 1,000 questions about financial products and services. It answers questions on topics including mortgages, credit cards, and how to dispute errors in a credit report. This resource is found at consumerfinance.gov/askcfpb/. We are also focusing on helping consumers build the skills to plan ahead. For example, our Paying for College set of tools helps students and their families compare what their college costs will be down the road as they decide where to pursue a college education. Our Owning a Home set of tools will help consumers shop for a mortgage loan by helping them understand what mortgages are available to them and easily make mortgage comparisons. The Money Smart for Older Adults curriculum, developed with the FDIC, includes resources to help people prevent elder financial exploitation and prepare financially for unexpected life events.

We are working with a broad range of partners to provide decision-making support in moments when consumers are most receptive to receiving information and developing financial decision-making skills. This includes integrating financial capability into other programs and services where consumers may be seeking assistance. We are also tailoring our approaches to financial decision-making circumstances, challenges, and opportunities for specific populations, including servicemembers and veterans, students and young adults, older Americans, and lower-income and other economically vulnerable Americans.

When Federal consumer financial protection law is violated, the Bureau's Supervision, Enforcement, and Fair Lending Division is committed to holding the responsible parties accountable. During this reporting period, the Bureau's enforcement efforts have helped secure orders for more than $1.6 billion in relief for consumers who fell victim to various violations of consumer financial protection laws. The Bureau has also continued to develop and refine its nationwide supervisory program for depository and nondepository financial institutions, through which those institutions are examined for compliance with Federal consumer financial protection law. Since the Bureau opened its doors in July 2011, nonpublic supervisory actions and self-reported violations in a number of program areas have resulted in more than $75 million in remediation for approximately 780,000 consumers. Initiatives during the reporting period of this report include a review of the existing internal examination report review processes and implementation of recommendations arising out of that review. On May 2, 2014, we issued updated templates for the supervisory letters and examination reports that we issue to institutions to explain what we found during our supervisory reviews or examinations.[4]

Continuing the CFPB's policy of transparency, the Bureau has released two editions of *Supervisory Highlights* during this reporting period, one focused entirely on the Bureau's fair lending supervisory activity in the indirect automobile lending market. This publications is intended to inform both industry and the public about the development of the Bureau's

---

[4] http://files.consumerfinance.gov/f/201405_cfpb_exam-report-supervisory-templates.pdf.

supervisory program and to discuss, in a manner consistent with the confidential nature of the supervisory process, broad trends in examination findings in key market or product areas.

The Bureau has also published new examination procedures and supervisory guidance documents, with other regulators where appropriate, to help institutions know what to expect and how to become, or remain, compliant with the law, including procedures or guidance with respect to brokers shifting to the "mini-correspondent" model,[5] mortgage servicing transfers,[6] and credit practices.[7]

Reasonable regulations are essential for protecting consumers from harmful practices and ensuring that consumer financial markets function in a fair, transparent, and competitive manner. The Research, Markets, and Regulations Division has focused its efforts on promoting markets in which consumers can shop effectively for financial products and services and are not subject to unfair, deceptive, or abusive acts or practices. During this reporting period, the Research and Markets teams released studies on medical debt and credit scores,[8] checking account overdrafts,[9] and manufactured-housing consumer finance.[10] The Regulations office issued regulations modifying and clarifying a number of rules implementing changes made by the Dodd-Frank Act to the laws governing various aspects of the mortgage market.

During this reporting period, the Bureau has published several proposed or final rules or requests for information under the Dodd-Frank Act, including amendments to the 2013 Mortgage Servicing and Ability-to-Repay rules. These proposed rules would provide an alternative small servicer definition for nonprofit entities that meet certain requirements, amend the existing exemption from the ability-to-repay rule for nonprofit entities that meet certain requirements, and provide a limited cure mechanism for the points and fees limit that

---

[5] http://files.consumerfinance.gov/f/201407_cfpb_guidance_mini-correspondent-lenders.pdf.

[6] http://files.consumerfinance.gov/f/201408_cfpb_bulletin_mortgage-servicing-transfer.pdf.

[7] Jointly with the FRB, FDIC, NCUA and OCC.
http://files.consumerfinance.gov/f/201408_cfpb_guidance_ffiec_credit-card-practices.pdf.

[8] http://files.consumerfinance.gov/f/201405_cfpb_report_data-point_medical-debt-credit-scores.pdf.

[9] http://files.consumerfinance.gov/f/201407_cfpb_report_data-point_overdrafts.pdf.

[10] http://files.consumerfinance.gov/f/201409_cfpb_report_manufactured-housing.pdf.

applies to qualified mortgages. The Bureau also issued a final rule amending the regulation defining larger participants of certain consumer financial product and service markets to add a new section to define larger participants of a market for international money transfers, and a proposed rule to add a new section to define larger participants in the automobile financing market.

To support the implementation of and industry compliance with its rules, the Bureau has published plain-language compliance guides and video presentations summarizing them, and it has actively engaged in discussions with industry about ways to achieve compliance.[11] The Bureau also continued its efforts to streamline, modernize, and harmonize financial regulations that it inherited from other agencies.

In addition to implementing the Dodd-Frank Act, the Bureau is exploring other areas where regulations may be needed to ensure that markets function properly and possibly harmful or inefficient practices are addressed. For example, the Bureau issued a proposal to amend Regulation P, which among other things, requires that financial institutions provide an annual disclosure of their privacy policies to their customers. The amendment would create an alternative delivery method for this annual disclosure, which financial institutions would be able to use under certain circumstances. Over the next six months, the Bureau will continue implementing the Dodd-Frank Act and using its regulatory authority to ensure that consumers have access to consumer financial markets that are fair, transparent, and competitive.

# 1.3   Building a great institution

The Bureau continues to grow and evolve as an institution. As of September 30, 2014, the CFPB team consisted of 1,443 employees working to carry out the Bureau's mission. It has worked to build a human and physical infrastructure that promotes – and will continue to promote – diversity, transparency, accountability, fairness, and service to the public. That includes:

- Demonstrating a strong commitment to openness and utilizing the Bureau's website to share information on its operations;

---

[11] http://www.consumerfinance.gov/guidance/#compliance.

- Recruiting highly-qualified, diverse personnel;
- Providing training and engagement opportunities for CFPB staff to improve skills, increase knowledge, and maintain excellence; and
- Further promoting diversity and inclusion in the CFPB's workforce and among its contractors, including through the Bureau's Office of Minority and Women Inclusion (OMWI).

The Bureau recognizes that the best way to serve consumers is to ensure that its workforce reflects the ideas, backgrounds, and experiences of the American public. OMWI supports the Bureau's mission by working with the offices of Human Capital and Equal Employment and Opportunity to continue building a diverse and inclusive workforce, with which the Bureau can foster broader and better thinking about how to approach markets.

We will continue working hard to ensure that the American people are treated fairly in the consumer financial marketplace. We encourage you to visit consumerfinance.gov for updates.

# 2. Consumer challenges in obtaining financial products and services

The challenges consumers face in navigating and obtaining financial products and services are a driving force behind the CFPB's efforts to make consumer financial markets work better. Listening and responding to consumers are integral components of our mission, and the Bureau provides numerous ways for consumers to make their voices heard.

## 2.1 Consumer concerns

The Bureau's long-term vision for consumer finance markets is one where consumer protections and business opportunities work in tandem, where financial firms lead through responsible business practices, and where educated consumers can make well-informed decisions. It is critical for the stability of the marketplace and the well-being of consumers to ensure that everyone is playing by the same rules.

As we continue to emerge from the continuing effects of the devastating financial crisis of 2008, we find that debt collection is central and cut across virtually all credit products: credit cards, mortgages, student loans, payday loans, and other consumer loans. Currently, about 30 million consumers – nearly one out of every ten Americans – are subject to debt collection, for amounts that average about $1,500 each.

Many companies in this industry play by the rules. But others cut corners and seek to gain an advantage by ignoring the rules. These bad actors are a detriment to every company that is faithfully following the law, and their actions harm consumers.

During the reporting period covered by this report, consumers have shared with the CFPB their experiences – positive and negative – with financial products and services, including debt collection. Consumers have the opportunity to provide the Bureau with such feedback through a variety of forums, including the "Tell Your Story" feature on the CFPB's website, and by participating in roundtables, town halls, and field hearings. This feedback is critical to our efforts to understand the challenges consumers face in obtaining the financial products and services they need.

With respect to credit cards, the first consumer financial product the Bureau accepted complaints about, many of the stories that consumers have shared with us over the past year through "Tell Your Story" indicate that consumers continue to experience issues with various aspects of credit card use. Consumers express frustration with the number of unwanted promotional offers they receive and with the issuance of unsolicited pre-approved credit cards. They also report account-related issues, including confusion over actual terms and fees versus those that were advertised and marketed to them. Others report their surprise when companies decrease their credit limit or close their account with little or no notice, as well as when these company actions negatively impact their credit scores. Consumers also express frustration with attempts to resolve billing disputes, payment issues, and fraud and ID theft related issues.

In addition to "Tell Your Story," consumers have opportunities to voice concerns and share their experiences in person at field hearings and public meetings, focused on particular consumer finance issues. During this reporting period, consumers and advocates have participated in large Bureau-sponsored public events in Chicago, IL; Washington, DC; New Orleans, LA; El Paso, TX; and Indianapolis, IN.[12] These events have drawn hundreds of participants, many of whom have shared their personal experiences with libraries, workplace financial education, mortgages, payday lending, mobile financial services, consumer finance complaints, and other consumer financial issues.

The CFPB's Office of Community Affairs has also hosted roundtable conversations with leaders of consumer, civil rights, community, housing, faith-based, student, and other organizations. The roundtables have provided opportunities for stakeholders to meet with Director Cordray,

---

[12] Between April 1, 2014 and September 30, 2014.

Deputy Director Antonakes, and other senior Bureau staff to share their first-hand perspectives on key consumer finance issues that affect their communities.

Collecting, investigating, and responding to consumer complaints are integral parts of the CFPB's work, as Congress set forth in the Dodd-Frank Act.[13] The Bureau hears directly from consumers about the challenges they face in the marketplace, brings their concerns to the attention of companies, and assists in addressing their complaints.

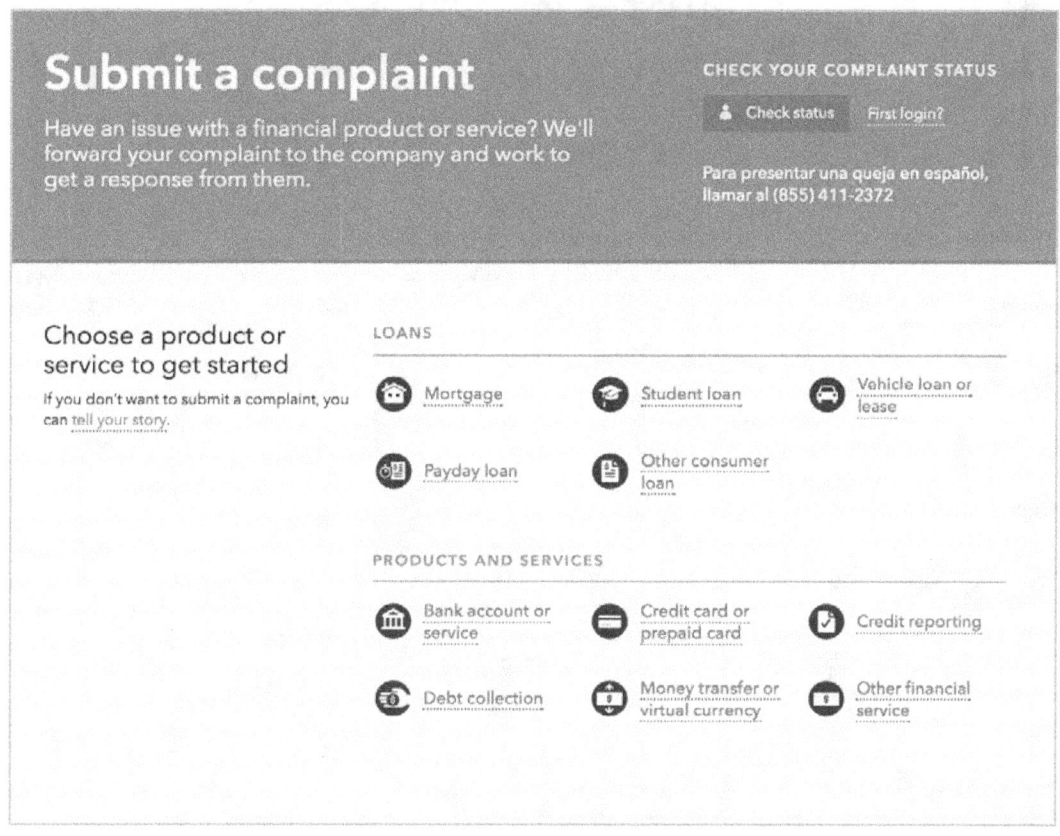

consumerfinance.gov/complaint

The CFPB began Consumer Response operations on July 21, 2011, by accepting consumer complaints about credit cards. The Bureau now accepts complaints about mortgages, bank accounts and services, student loans, vehicle and other consumer loans, credit reporting, money

---

[13] *See* Dodd-Frank Act, Pub. L. No. 111-203, Sec. 1021(c)(2).

transfers, debt collection, payday loans, prepaid cards, additional nonbank products (including debt settlement services, credit repair services, and pawn and title loans), and digital currency. The CFPB continues to work toward expanding its complaint-handling capacity and plans to include other products and services. Consumers may also contact the CFPB with questions about other products and services. The Bureau answers questions and refers consumers to other regulators or additional resources as appropriate.

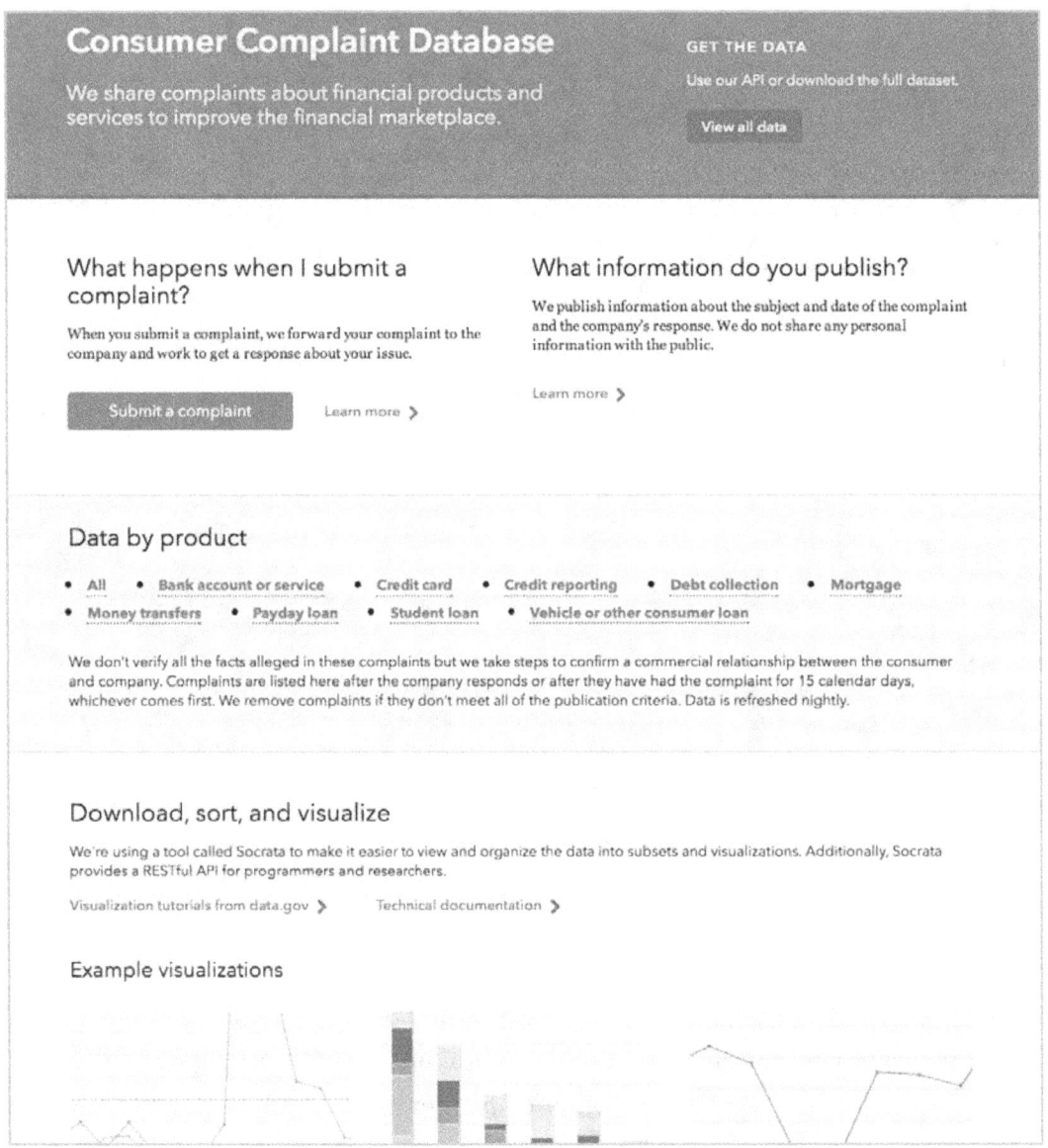

consumerfinance.gov/complaintdatabase

Information about consumer complaints is available to the public, through the Bureau's public Consumer Complaint Database, launched on June 19, 2012. It was initially populated with credit card complaints received on and after June 1, 2012, and has been expanded over time:

- October 2012: added credit card complaints dating back to December 1, 2011;

- March 2013: added mortgage complaints dating back to December 1, 2011, bank account and service complaints, student loan complaints, vehicle and other consumer loan complaints, all dating back to March 1, 2012;

- May 2013: added credit reporting complaints dating back to October 22, 2012 and money transfer complaints dating back to April 4, 2013;

- November 2013: added debt collection complaints dating back to July 10, 2013;

- July 2014: added payday loan complaints dating back to November 6, 2013.

A complaint is listed in the database when the company responds to the complaint confirming a commercial relationship with the consumer, or after the company has had the complaint for 15 days, whichever comes first. Complaints can be removed if they do not meet all of the publication criteria.

The database updates nightly, and contains certain individual complaint-level data collected by the CFPB, including the type of complaint, the date of submission, the consumer's zip code, and the company that the complaint concerns. The database also includes information about the actions taken by a company in response to a complaint – whether the company's response was timely, how the company responded, and whether the consumer disputed the company's response. The database does not include confidential information about consumers' identities. Web-based and user-friendly features of the database include the ability to filter data based on specific search criteria, to aggregate data in various ways, such as by complaint type, company, zip code, date, or any combination of available variables, and to download data. Information from the database has been shared and evaluated on social media and using other new applications.

The Bureau continues to evaluate, as noted above, the release of consumer narratives, as well as the potential for normalization of data to make comparisons easier, and the expansion of functionality to improve user experience.

## 2.1.1   How the CFPB handles complaints

In keeping with the CFPB's statutory responsibility and its commitment to accountability, the following pages provide an overview of the handling and analysis of complaints received by the Bureau from October 1, 2013 through September 30, 2014.[14]

The CFPB's Consumer Response team screens all complaints submitted by consumers based on several criteria, including whether the complaint falls within the Bureau's primary enforcement authority, whether the complaint is complete, and whether the complaint is duplicative of a prior submission by the same consumer. Screened complaints are forwarded via a secure web portal to the appropriate company.[15] The company reviews the information, communicates with the consumer as needed, and determines what action to take in response. The company then reports back to the consumer and the CFPB via the secure company portal, and the Bureau invites the consumer to review the response and provide feedback. Consumer Response reviews the feedback consumers provide about company responses, using this information along with other information such as the timeliness of the company's response, for example, to help prioritize complaints for investigation.[16] Consumers who have submitted complaints to the Bureau through Consumer Response can log onto the secure consumer portal available on the CFPB's website, or call a toll-free number, to receive status updates, provide additional information, and review responses provided to the consumer by the company.

---

[14] While the reporting period for this Semi-Annual Report is six months, Dodd-Frank Act § 1016(c)(4) requires "an analysis of complaints about consumer financial products or services that the Bureau has received and collected in its central database on complaints during the preceding year." Therefore, this section reports on the time period October 1, 2013 through September 30, 2014.

[15] If a particular complaint does not involve a product or market that is within the Bureau's enforcement authority, or that is not currently being handled by the Bureau, Consumer Response refers it to the appropriate regulator.

[16] The CFPB requests that companies respond to complaints within 15 calendar days. If a complaint cannot be closed within 15 calendar days, a company may indicate that its work on the complaint is "In progress" and provide a final response within 60 calendar days.

 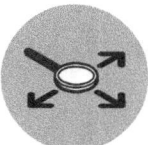    

| Complaint submitted | > | Review and route | > | Company response | > | Consumer review | > | Review and investigate | > | Analyze and report |

Throughout this process, subject-matter experts help monitor certain complaints. For example, the Office of Servicemember Affairs coordinates with Consumer Response on complaints filed by servicemembers or their spouses and dependents.

The Bureau continually strives to improve data quality and protect sensitive information, while increasingly making data about the complaints the CFPB receives available through reports to Congress and the public, and by sharing certain data with the public through the Consumer Complaint Database.

## 2.1.2 Complaints received by the CFPB

Between October 1, 2013 and September 30, 2014, the CFPB received approximately 240,600 consumer complaints.[17] Approximately 65% of all consumer complaints were submitted through the CFPB's website and 10% via telephone calls. Referrals accounted for 15% of all complaints received, with the remainder submitted by mail, email, and fax.[18]

---

[17] Unless otherwise noted or the context suggests otherwise, the various tables and complaint tabulations appearing herein cover this period.

[18] This analysis excludes multiple complaints submitted by a given consumer on the same issue and whistleblower tips. All data are current as of September 30, 2014. Since launching Consumer Response operations on July 21, 2011 through September 30, 2014, the CFPB received approximately 460,700 consumer complaints.

**FIGURE 1:** CONSUMER COMPLAINTS BY PRODUCT

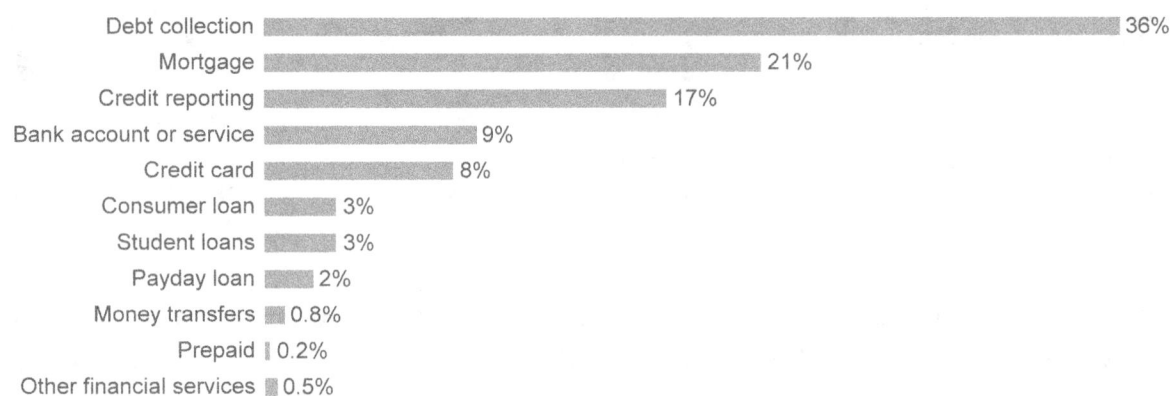

The Dodd-Frank Act created the Office of Servicemember Affairs to address the specific challenges faced by servicemembers, veterans, and their families (collectively "servicemembers"). It monitors complaints from servicemembers in conjunction with Consumer Response. Between October 1, 2013 and September 30, 2014, approximately 16,000 complaints were submitted by servicemembers.

**FIGURE 2:** SERVICEMEMBER COMPLAINTS BY PRODUCT

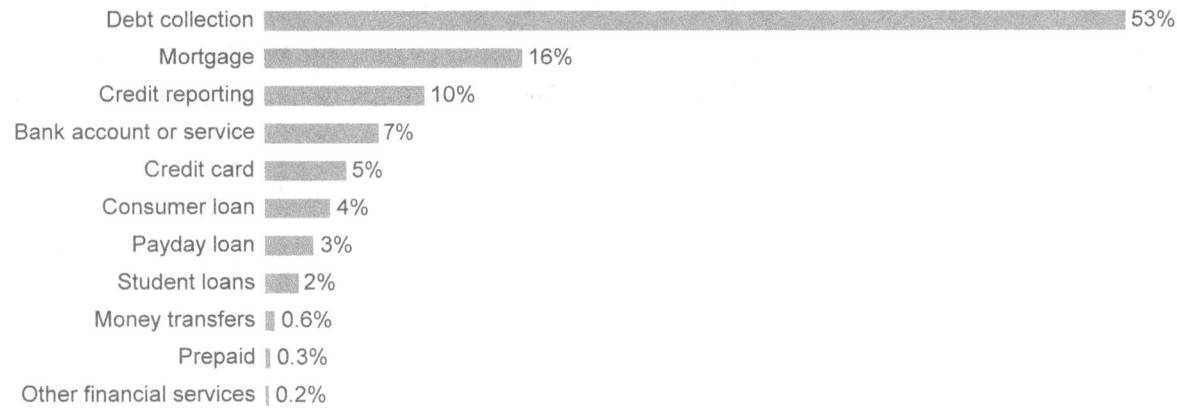

The tables and figures presented below show complaints by type, actions taken, company responses, and consumers' feedback about company responses.[19]

---

[19] Percentages may not sum to 100% due to rounding.

# Consumers' debt collection complaints

Figure 3 and Table 1 show the types of debt collection complaints reported by consumers for the approximately 86,900 debt collection complaints the CFPB has received.

**FIGURE 3:** TYPES OF DEBT COLLECTION COMPLAINTS REPORTED BY CONSUMERS

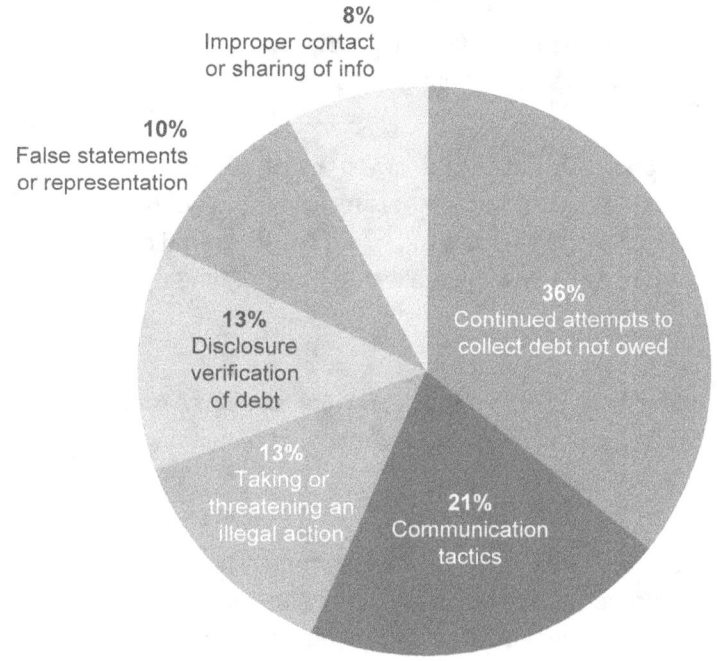

**TABLE 1:** TYPES OF DEBT COLLECTION COMPLAINTS REPORTED BY CONSUMERS

| Types of Debt Collection Complaints | % |
| --- | --- |
| Continued attempts to collect debt not owed (Debt was discharged in bankruptcy, debt resulted from identity theft, debt was paid, debt is not mine) | 36% |
| Communication tactics (Frequent or repeated calls, called outside of 8am-9pm, used obscene, profane or other abusive language, threatened to take legal action, called after sent written cease of communication notice) | 21% |
| Taking/threatening an illegal action (Threatened to arrest me or take me to jail if I do not pay, threatened to sue me on debt that is too old to be sued on, sued me without properly notifying me of lawsuit, sued me where I did not live or did not sign for the debt, attempted to/collected exempt funds, seized or attempted to seize property) | 13% |
| Disclosure verification of debt (Did not receive notice of right to dispute, not enough information to verify debt, did not disclose communication was an attempt to collect a debt) | 13% |
| False statements or representation (Attempted to collect wrong amount, impersonated attorney, law enforcement or government official, indicated committing crime by not paying debt, indicated should not respond to lawsuit) | 10% |
| Improper contact or sharing of information (Contacted me after I asked not to, contacted my employer, contacted me instead of my attorney, talked to a third party about my debt) | 8% |
| **Total debt collection complaints** | **100%** |

As the table illustrates, the most common type of debt collection complaint is about continued attempts to collect a debt that is not owed. In many of these cases, the attempt to collect the debt is not itself the problem; rather, consumers argue that the calculation of the underlying debt is inaccurate or unfair. In other cases, the consumer's complaint centers on the credit reporting of the debt. These complaints, which are often mirrored by credit reporting complaints submitted to the Bureau, indicate that consumers frequently only learn about debt collection accounts when they check their credit reports.

Another common type of complaint, related to consumers' questions about the underlying debt, involves verification of the debt. In these complaints, consumers ask the debt collection company to provide them with validation or verification of the underlying debt. Consumers are generally seeking documentation that they were the ones who signed the contract underlying the debt in question. Consumers, however, report that collectors do not provide them with information that the consumers believe they should provide.

Complaints about communication tactics, particularly telephone collections, are another common type of consumer complaint. Consumers complain about telephone collections which are too frequent and which come at inconvenient times of the day. They also complain about debt collectors calling their place of employment or third parties. The most common telephone collection related complaint is when a consumer gets a call about another person's debt. Sometimes the call is for someone with a similar name. More often, it appears the consumer's phone number has mistakenly been attached to another person's account. In most of these cases, it appears that consumers are submitting their complaint to the CFPB after repeated failed attempts to inform the company calling them that the debtor is not located at that number.

# Consumers' mortgage complaints

Figure 4 and Table 2 show the types of mortgage complaints reported by consumers for the approximately 50,400 mortgage complaints the CFPB has received.

**FIGURE 4:** TYPES OF MORTGAGE COMPLAINTS REPORTED BY CONSUMERS

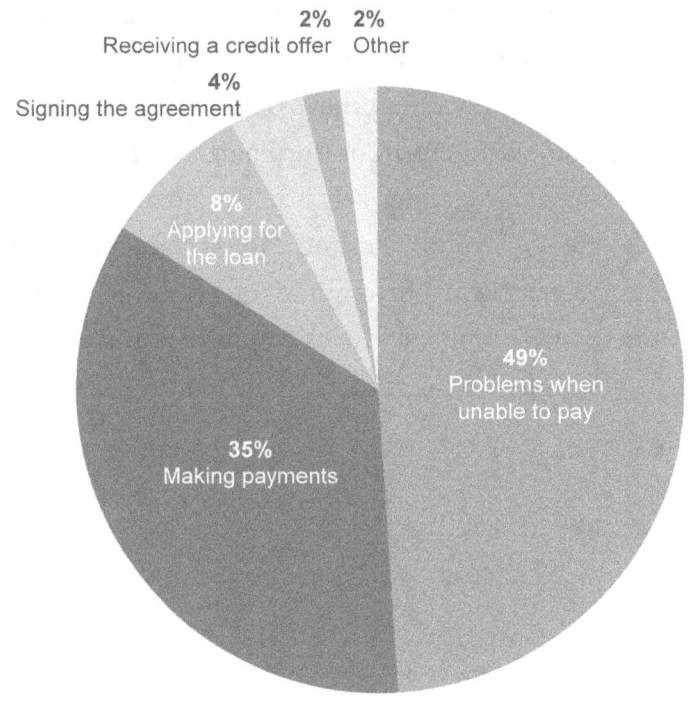

**TABLE 2:** TYPES OF MORTGAGE COMPLAINTS REPORTED BY CONSUMERS

| Types of Mortgage Complaints | % |
|---|---|
| Problems when you are unable to pay (Loan modification, collection, foreclosure) | 49% |
| Making payments (Loan servicing, payments, escrow accounts) | 35% |
| Applying for the loan (Application, originator, mortgage broker) | 8% |
| Signing the agreement (Settlement process and costs) | 4% |
| Receiving a credit offer (Credit decision/Underwriting) | 2% |
| Other | 2% |
| **Total mortgage complaints** | **100%** |

The most common type of mortgage complaint involves problems consumers face when they are unable to make payments, such as issues relating to loan modifications, collections, or foreclosures. Consumers with successfully completed loan modifications have complained that some servicers do not amend derogatory credit reporting accrued by consumers during trial periods – even when documents provided to the consumers by servicers indicated that they would do so. Consumers seeking short sales have reported that second-lien holders refuse to accept or subordinate in a short sale, whereas some consumers who do obtain a short sale have concerns with the loan account being incorrectly reported as a foreclosure. Consumers facing foreclosure have expressed concern and confusion about fees assessed in connection with the foreclosure process. The fees often seem to represent a substantial barrier to a consumer's ability to reinstate the loan and avoid foreclosure, as many servicers will not roll the fees into the loan balance. Consumers are then required to pay hundreds or thousands of dollars, in addition to the loan reinstatement amount, to avoid foreclosure, and the amount of fees the consumer must pay to reinstate the loan can be confusing. Finally, foreclosure fees are sometimes listed as one line-item on a reinstatement quote, with no itemization provided unless the consumer specifically requests more information on what fees are being assessed.

Other common types of mortgage complaints address issues related to making payments, including loan servicing, or escrow accounts. For example, consumers express concern over difficulties they experience when the servicing of their loans are transferred, including complaints about fees charged by the prior servicer, unexplained escrow deficiencies, issues with the new servicer accepting the previous servicer's modification, and communication between the old and new servicer, especially when loss mitigation efforts are ongoing.

For consumers applying for a mortgage loan, consumers raise issues related to interest rate-lock agreements, such as lenders refusing to honor rate-locks, or assessing penalties when the loan does not close.

## Consumers' credit reporting complaints

Figure 5 and Table 3 show the types of credit reporting complaints reported by consumers for the approximately 40,600 credit reporting complaints the CFPB has received.

**FIGURE 5:** TYPES OF CREDIT REPORTING COMPLAINTS REPORTED BY CONSUMERS

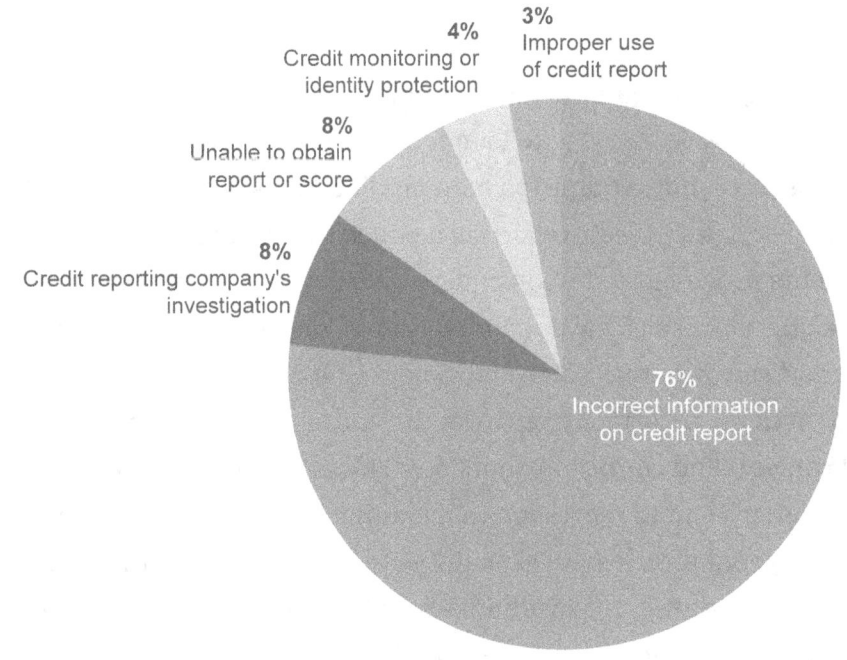

**TABLE 3:** TYPES OF CREDIT REPORTING COMPLAINTS REPORTED BY CONSUMERS

| Types of Credit Reporting Complaints | % |
| --- | --- |
| Incorrect information on credit report (Information is not mine, Account terms, Account status, Personal information, Public record, Reinserted previously deleted information) | 76% |
| Credit reporting company's investigation (Investigation took too long, Did not get proper notice of investigation status or results, Did not receive adequate help over the phone, Problem with statement of dispute) | 8% |
| Unable to get my credit report or credit score (Problem getting free annual report, Problem getting report or credit score) | 8% |
| Credit monitoring or identity protection services (Problem cancelling or closing account, Billing dispute, Receiving unwanted marketing or advertising, Account or product terms and changes, Problem with fraud alerts) | 4% |
| Improper use of my credit report (Report improperly shared by credit reporting company, Received marketing offers after opting out, Report provided to employer without written authorization) | 3% |
| **Total credit reporting complaints** | **100%** |

This table illustrates that the most common type of credit reporting complaint is about incorrect information appearing on the consumer's credit report, such as information that does not belong to the consumer, incorrect account status, and incorrect personal information.

Another common type of complaint is about issues with credit reporting companies' investigations of information disputed by consumers. Consumers report that credit reporting companies sometimes return findings on their disputes within only a few days, and consumers question the depth and validity of such quick investigations. Additionally, consumers report frustration when they have submitted documentation that they believe proves that the information provided by the data furnisher was inaccurate, but no change is made to their credit report.

# Consumers' bank account and service complaints

Figure 6 and Table 4 show types of bank account and service complaints, such as complaints about checking and savings accounts, reported by consumers for the approximately 21,700 bank account and service complaints received by the CFPB.

**FIGURE 6:**   TYPES OF BANK ACCOUNT AND SERVICE COMPLAINTS REPORTED BY CONSUMERS

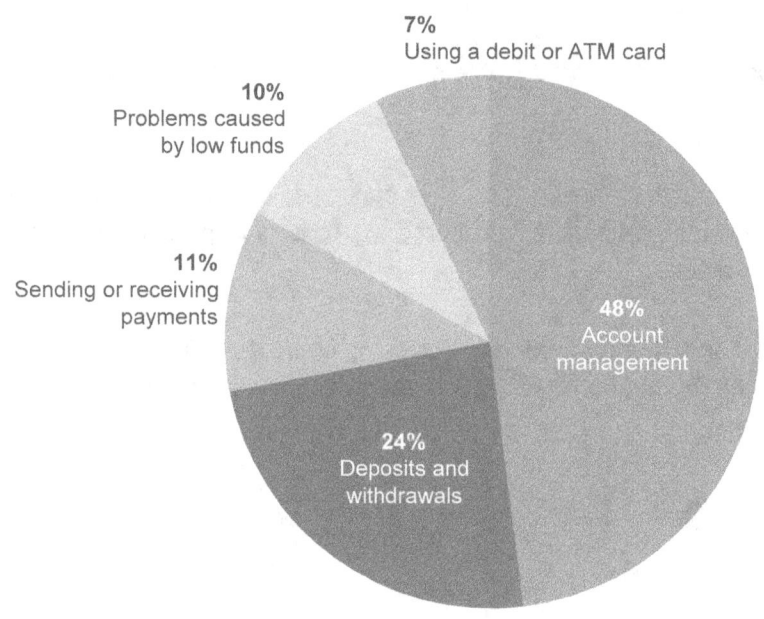

**TABLE 4:** TYPES OF BANK ACCOUNT AND SERVICE COMPLAINTS REPORTED BY CONSUMERS

| Types of Bank Account and Service Complaints | % |
|---|---|
| Account opening, closing, or management (Confusing marketing, denial, disclosure, fees, closure, interest, statements, joint accounts) | 48% |
| Deposits and withdrawals (Availability of deposits, withdrawal problems and penalties, unauthorized transactions, check cashing, payroll deposit problems, lost or missing funds, transaction holds) | 24% |
| Making or receiving payments, sending money to others (Problems with payments by check, card, phone or online, unauthorized or fraudulent transactions, money/wire transfers) | 11% |
| Problems caused by my funds being low (Overdraft fees, late fees, bounced checks, credit reporting) | 10% |
| Using a debit or ATM card (Disputed transaction, unauthorized card use, ATM or debit card fees, ATM problems) | 7% |
| **Total bank account and service complaints** | **100%** |

As the table illustrates, the most common type of bank account and service complaint relates to opening, closing, or managing the account. These complaints address issues such as account maintenance fees, legal processing fees for judgments and levies, changes in account terms, confusing marketing, early withdrawal penalties for certificates of deposit, and involuntary account closures. Other common complaints relate to deposit and withdrawal issues, such as transaction holds, the company's right to offset deposit accounts, and unauthorized debit card charges. In this area, many consumers are frustrated by companies' handling of error disputes and requests to stop payment on preauthorized electronic debits. Another common type of complaint relates to problems caused by a consumer's funds being low, including overdraft fees, bounced checks, charged-off accounts, and negative reporting to credit reporting agencies. In this area, many consumers are frustrated by the way some companies appear to manipulate the order in which deposits and withdrawals are posted to consumers' accounts to maximize overdraft fees.

## Consumers' credit card complaints

Table 5 shows the most common types of credit card complaints that the CFPB has received as reported by consumers. About 74% of the approximately 18,300 credit card complaints fell into these 10 categories.

TABLE 5:   MOST COMMON CREDIT CARD COMPLAINTS REPORTED BY CONSUMERS

| Complaint | % |
|---|---|
| Billing disputes | 17% |
| Other | 13% |
| Identity theft/Fraud/Embezzlement | 11% |
| Closing/Cancelling account | 7% |
| APR or interest rate | 6% |
| Advertising and marketing | 5% |
| Customer service/Customer relations | 4% |
| Late fee | 4% |
| Delinquent account | 4% |
| Transaction issue | 3% |
| **Credit card complaints in top 10 types** | **74%** |

As the table illustrates, billing disputes are the most common type of credit card complaint. Consumers continue to be confused and frustrated by the process and by their limited ability to challenge inaccuracies on their monthly credit card billing statements. For example, some consumers realize only after their claim has been denied that they needed to notify their credit card companies within 60 days of any billing errors. In other cases, consumers are not aware that companies typically do not stop a merchant charge once the cardholder has authorized it, or do not override a merchant's "no-return policy." Other common types of credit card complaints relate to identity theft, fraud, or embezzlement; closing or cancelling an account; and annual percentage rates or interest rates.

The Bureau generally has relied on the consumer's characterization of his or her complaint to identify its nature for analytical purposes. However, the CFPB's experience to date suggests that consumers may have differing interpretations of what these categories mean. For example, one consumer might choose to categorize a problem as a billing dispute, while another might identify the same issue as a concern with a provider's setting or changing of an interest rate. To improve our reporting on the data we receive, the Bureau is evaluating the use of these categories by consumers to date and developing simplified identification to promote more consistent categorization of complaints.

## Consumers' consumer loan complaints

Figure 7 and Table 6 show the types of consumer loan complaints, such as complaints about installment loans, vehicle loans and leases, personal lines of credit, and pawn and title loans reported by consumers for the approximately 8,200 consumer loan complaints received by the CFPB.[20]

---

[20] The Bureau began handling complaints about pawn and title loans as part of the consumer loan complaint category on July 19, 2014.

**FIGURE 7:**   TYPES OF CONSUMER LOAN COMPLAINTS REPORTED BY CONSUMERS

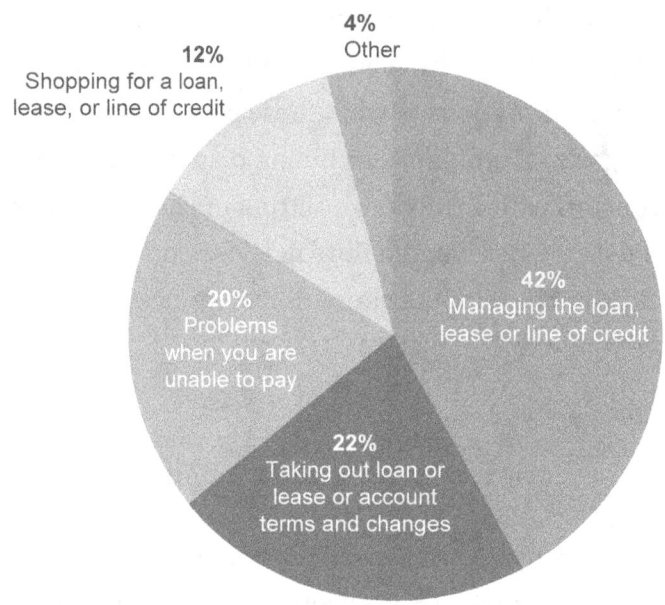

**TABLE 6:** TYPES OF CONSUMER LOAN COMPLAINTS REPORTED BY CONSUMERS

| Types of Consumer Loan Complaints | % |
|---|---|
| Managing the loan, lease, or line of credit (Billing, late fees, damage or loss, insurance (GAP, credit, etc.), credit reporting, privacy) | 42% |
| Taking out the loan or lease / Account terms and changes (Term changes (mid-deal changes, changes after closing, rates, fees, etc.), required add-on products, trade-in payoff, fraud) | 22% |
| Problems when you are unable to pay (Debt collection, repossession, set-off from bank account, deficiency, bankruptcy, default) | 20% |
| Shopping for a loan, lease, or line of credit (Sales tactics or pressure, credit denial, confusing advertising or marketing) | 12% |
| Other (Charged fees or interest I did not expect, identity theft/fraud/embezzlement, billing disputes, credit reporting, other) | 4% |
| **Total consumer loan complaints** | **100%** |

The table illustrates that the most common type of consumer loan complaint pertains to managing the loan, lease, or line of credit. Other common types of complaints address problems consumers have when taking out the loan or lease, such as term changes, and problems when they are unable to pay, including issues related to debt collection, bankruptcy, and default.

## Consumers' student loan complaints

Figure 8 and Table 7 show the types of student loan complaints reported by consumers for the approximately 6,200 student loan complaints received by the CFPB.[21]

---

[21] Prior to December 18, 2013, consumers submitting student loan complaints could select from three types of complaint categories: *Getting a loan*, *Repaying your loan*, and *Problems when you are unable to pay*. Beginning on December 18, 2013, the student loan complaint form was updated to make it easier for consumers submitting a complaint to categorize the problems they are having with their student loan. Consumers now select from the

**FIGURE 8:** TYPES OF STUDENT LOAN COMPLAINTS REPORTED BY CONSUMERS

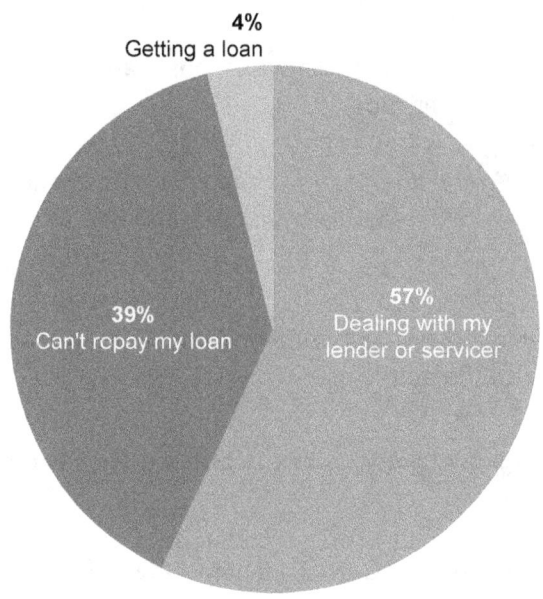

following three types of complaint categories: *Getting a loan, Can't pay my loan,* and *Dealing with my lender or servicer.* This report includes the types of complaints submitted under both the original and updated forms. The *Repaying your loan* category is under *Dealing with my lender or servicer,* and *Problems when you are unable to pay* is under *Can't repay my loan.*

**TABLE 7:** TYPES OF STUDENT LOAN COMPLAINTS REPORTED BY CONSUMERS

| Types of Student Loan Complaints | % |
|---|---|
| Dealing with my lender or servicer (Making payments, getting information about my loan, managing my account) | 57% |
| Can't repay my loan (Deferment, forbearance, default, bankruptcy, payment plan, refinancing) | 39% |
| Getting a loan (Confusing terms, rates, denial, confusing advertising or marketing, sales tactics or pressure, financial aid services, recruiting) | 4% |
| **Total student loan complaints** | **100%** |

The most common type of student loan complaint relates to dealing with a lender or servicer and includes issues such as making payments, getting information about a loan, and managing an account. Consumers raised concerns about a range of servicing problems, including payment processing problems, challenges obtaining necessary documentation about their private student loans, difficulty obtaining accurate information about their loan status and repayment options, and obstacles to accessing basic account information. Another common type of complaint addresses problems consumers confront when they are unable to pay, such as issues related to default, debt collection, and bankruptcy. Consumers report that they continue to struggle with the limited affordable payment options permitted in their loan agreements. Specifically, consumers say they are unable to refinance or restructure the repayment terms of their loan, either to lower monthly payments during periods of financial hardship, or to improve existing terms based upon the consumer's improved credit profile and credit-worthiness.

## Consumers' money transfer complaints

Figure 9 and Table 8 show the types of money transfer complaints reported by consumers for the approximately 1,900 money transfer complaints the CFPB has received.[22]

---

[22] The Bureau began handling complaints about virtual currency as part of the money transfer complaint category on August 11, 2014.

**FIGURE 9:**  TYPES OF MONEY TRANSFER COMPLAINTS REPORTED BY CONSUMERS

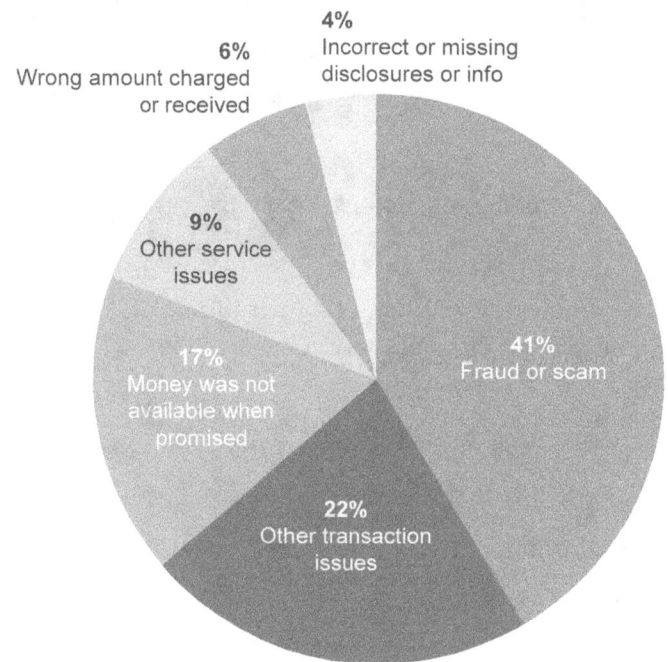

**TABLE 8:**   TYPES OF MONEY TRANSFER COMPLAINTS REPORTED BY CONSUMERS

| Types of Money Transfer Complaints | % |
|---|---|
| Fraud or scam | 41% |
| Other transaction issues (Unauthorized transaction, cancellation, refund, etc.) | 22% |
| Money was not available when promised | 17% |
| Other service issues (Advertising or marketing, pricing, privacy, etc.) | 9% |
| Wrong amount charged or received (Transfer amounts, fees, exchange rates, taxes, etc.) | 6% |
| Incorrect/missing disclosures or info | 4% |
| **Total money transfer complaints** | **100%** |

This table illustrates that the most common type of money transfer complaint is about fraud or scams. In these cases, the consumer is prompted to send funds as a result of a scam, and someone other than the consumer's intended recipient ultimately receives the funds. For example, consumers often complain that they were prompted to transfer funds in response to a request for help from a family member or friend, for the purchase of goods or services, the rental of an apartment, a loan, a job opportunity, or to pay taxes on lottery earnings. In response to such complaints, companies engaged in money transfers suggest that they have no liability when someone other than the intended recipient receives the funds, as long as the company complied with its policies and procedures and the minimum identification requirements were satisfied by the recipient. Other common complaints involve issues with other aspects of transactions, such as unauthorized transactions, and refusals to cancel or provide refunds when the consumers believe the company should provide them.

## Consumers' prepaid cards complaints

Figure 10 and Table 9 show the types of prepaid card complaints reported by consumers for the approximately 400 prepaid card complaints the CFPB has received. [23]

FIGURE 10:   TYPES OF PREPAID CARD COMPLAINTS REPORTED BY CONSUMERS

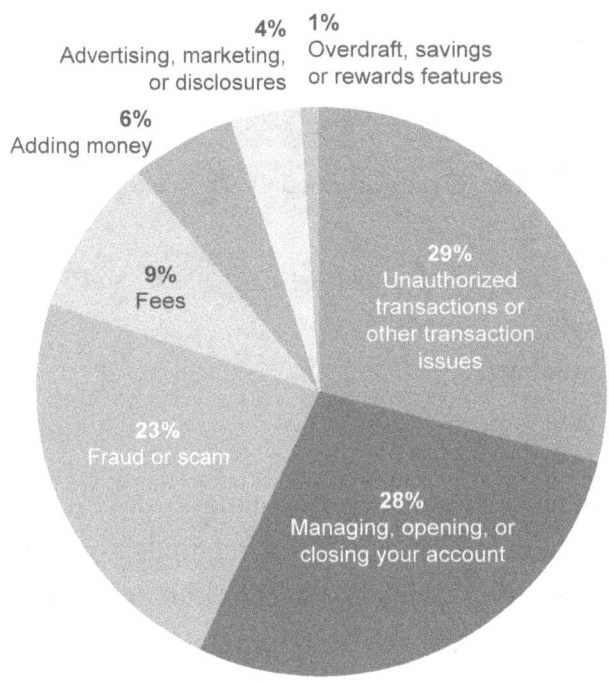

---

[23] CFPB began accepting complaints about prepaid cards on July 19, 2014.

**TABLE 9:** TYPES OF PREPAID CARD COMPLAINTS REPORTED BY CONSUMERS

| Types of Prepaid Card Complaints | % |
|---|---|
| Unauthorized transactions or other transaction issues | 29% |
| Managing, opening, or closing your account | 28% |
| Fraud or scam | 23% |
| Fees | 9% |
| Adding money | 6% |
| Advertising, marketing, or disclosures | 4% |
| Overdraft, savings or rewards features | 1% |
| **Total prepaid complaints** | **100%** |

Of the approximately 400 prepaid card complaints submitted by consumers, approximately 29% dealt with transactional issues in managing a prepaid card account. Approximately 23% of prepaid card complaints covered misleading advertising or scams, while approximately 9% covered complaints on account fees.

The most common type of prepaid card complaint was about unauthorized transactions or other transaction issues. Another common type of complaint involved managing, opening, or closing a prepaid card account. Consumers also commonly complained about frauds and scams in relation to prepaid cards.

The remaining complaints involved issues with adding money to a reloadable prepaid card, dealing with misleading adverting or marketing, and incurring overdraft fees or not being properly compensated on rewards.

## Other financial services complaints

Figure 11 and Table 10 show the types of other financial services complaints reported by consumers for the approximately 300 other financial services complaints the CFPB has received.[24]

FIGURE 11:  TYPES OF OTHER FINANCIAL SERVICES COMPLAINTS REPORTED BY CONSUMERS

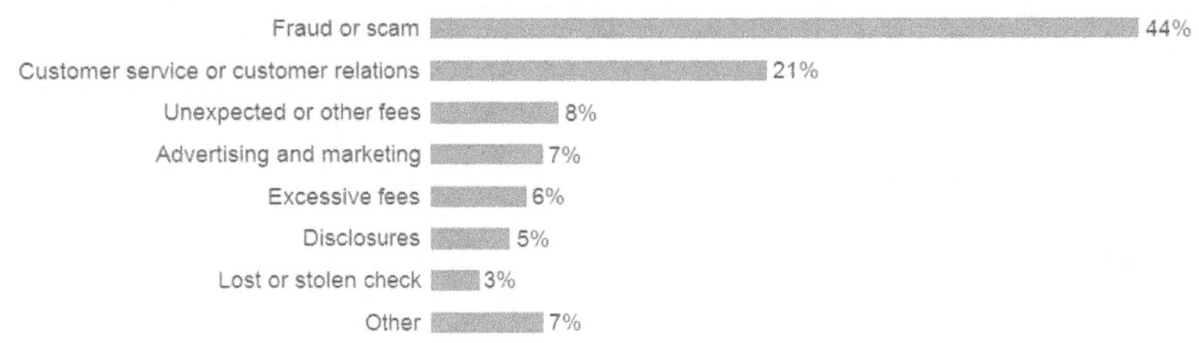

---

[24] CFPB began accepting complaints about check cashing, credit repair, debt settlement, foreign currency exchange, money orders, refund anticipation checks, and travelers' and cashiers' checks on July 19, 2014.

| Types of Other Financial Services Complaints | % |
|---|---|
| Fraud or scam | 44% |
| Customer service or customer relations | 21% |
| Unexpected or other fees | 8% |
| Advertising and marketing | 7% |
| Excessive fees | 6% |
| Disclosures | 5% |
| Lost or stolen check | 3% |
| Other | 7% |
| **Total other financial services complaints** | **100%** |

Of the 300 other financial services complaints submitted by consumers, approximately 51% dealt with misleading advertising or scams. Approximately 21%of complaints covered insufficient customer service, while approximately 14% of complaints dealt with excessive or unexpected fees while using other financial services.

The most common type of other financial services complaint was about fraud and scams. Another common complaint dealt with insufficient customer service.

The remaining complaints for other financial services involved issues with unexpected fees or excessive fees, dealing with misleading adverting or marketing, improper disclosures and lost or stolen checks.

## How companies respond to consumer complaints

Approximately 147,900 (or 61%) of all complaints received between October 1, 2013 and September 30, 2014 were sent by Consumer Response to companies for review and response.[25] Table 11 shows how companies responded to these complaints during this time period.

Company responses include descriptions of steps taken or that will be taken, communications received from the consumer, any follow-up actions or planned follow-up actions, and a categorization of the response. Response category options include "closed with monetary relief," "closed with non-monetary relief," "closed with explanation," "closed," "in progress," and other administrative options. "Monetary relief" is defined as objective, measurable, and verifiable monetary relief to the consumer as a direct result of the steps taken or that will be taken in response to the complaint. "Closed with non-monetary relief" indicates that the steps taken by the company in response to the complaint did not result in monetary relief to the consumer that is objective, measurable, and verifiable, but may have addressed some or all of the consumer's complaint involving non-monetary requests. "Non-monetary relief" is defined as other objective and verifiable relief to the consumer as a direct result of the steps taken or that will be taken in response to the complaint. "Closed with explanation" indicates that the steps taken by the company in response to the complaint included an explanation that was tailored to the individual consumer's complaint. For example, this category would be used if the explanation substantively meets the consumer's desired resolution or explains why no further action will be taken. "Closed" indicates that the company closed the complaint without relief – monetary or non-monetary – or explanation. Consumers are given the option to review and dispute all company closure responses.

Companies have responded to approximately 93% of complaints[26] sent to them and report having closed 90% of the complaints sent to them. Table 11 shows how companies have responded to consumer complaints, and Table 12 shows untimely company responses as a percentage of complaints sent to companies for response.

---

[25] The remaining complaints have been referred to other regulatory agencies (24%), found to be incomplete (9%), or are pending with the consumer or the CFPB (2% and 3%, respectively).

[26] Companies have responded to approximately 138,200 of the 147,900 sent to them for response.

**TABLE 11:** HOW COMPANIES HAVE RESPONDED TO CONSUMER COMPLAINTS[27]

| | Closed with monetary relief | Closed with non-monetary relief | Closed with explanation | Closed (without relief or explanation) | Administrative response | Company reviewing | Company did not provide a timely response |
|---|---|---|---|---|---|---|---|
| Debt collection | 2% | 17% | 66% | 3% | 1% | 3% | 8% |
| Mortgage | 2% | 4% | 80% | 2% | 4% | 5% | 3% |
| Credit reporting | 1% | 34% | 59% | 0% | 1% | 4% | 0% |
| Bank account or service | 21% | 5% | 64% | 3% | 2% | 4% | 1% |
| Credit card | 22% | 10% | 59% | 0% | 2% | 4% | 3% |
| Consumer loan | 7% | 7% | 74% | 1% | 1% | 6% | 4% |
| Student loans | 7% | 10% | 73% | 0% | 1% | 6% | 3% |
| Money transfers | 13% | 3% | 73% | 1% | 2% | 7% | 2% |
| Payday loan | 4% | 5% | 67% | 1% | 4% | 5% | 13% |
| Other financial services | 3% | 0% | 4% | 7% | 66% | 0% | 20% |
| Prepaid | 25% | 4% | 53% | 1% | 1% | 11% | 4% |
| **All** | 6% | 13% | 68% | 2% | 2% | 4% | 4% |

[27] While companies' responses under previous categorizations were maintained, for operational and reporting purposes, responses categorized as "full resolution provided," "partial resolution provided," and "closed with relief" are considered a subset of "closed with monetary relief," and responses categorized as "no resolution provided" and "closed without relief" are categorized as "closed with explanation."

**TABLE 12:** UNTIMELY COMPANY RESPONSES AS A PERCENTAGE OF COMPLAINTS SENT TO COMPANY

| | Closed with monetary relief | Closed with non-monetary relief | Closed with explanation | Closed (without relief or explanation) | Administrative response | Company reviewing | No response |
|---|---|---|---|---|---|---|---|
| Debt collection | 1% | 9% | 65% | 6% | 4% | 2% | 12% |
| Mortgage | 1% | 2% | 75% | 4% | 8% | 2% | 8% |
| Credit reporting | 2% | 11% | 76% | 2% | 5% | 2% | 2% |
| Bank account or service | 13% | 3% | 67% | 8% | 5% | 0% | 4% |
| Credit card | 22% | 7% | 64% | 1% | 2% | 2% | 2% |
| Consumer loan | 7% | 4% | 77% | 2% | 2% | 2% | 7% |
| Student loans | 2% | 5% | 84% | 2% | 1% | 6% | 1% |
| Money transfers | 19% | 0% | 63% | 4% | 7% | 0% | 7% |
| Payday loan | 2% | 2% | 39% | 5% | 16% | 0% | 35% |
| Other financial services | 3% | 3% | 77% | 6% | 0% | 3% | 9% |
| Prepaid | 17% | 0% | 83% | 0% | 0% | 0% | 0% |
| **All** | **4%** | **7%** | **67%** | **5%** | **5%** | **2%** | **10%** |

After Consumer Response forwards complaints to companies, the company has 15 days to respond and 60 days to provide a final response, where applicable. Company responses provided outside of these windows are deemed untimely. As shown in Table 12, consumers eventually received responses in 90% of cases where companies did not respond to the complaint in a timely manner. Where companies eventually responded to the consumer, most often they provided a response of "Closed with explanation". However, 10% of complaints with untimely company responses never received a response. Payday loan complaints were the most likely to receive no response, with 35% of complaints with an untimely company response never receiving a response.

Companies have the option to report an amount of monetary relief, where applicable. As of September 30, 2014, companies provided relief amounts in response to more than 8,700 complaints. For companies which have reported monetary relief, the median amount of relief reported was $143; however, the amount varies by product. For the more than 3,130 bank account and service complaints where companies provided a relief amount, the median amount of relief reported was approximately $105. For the approximately 3,120 credit card complaints where companies provided a relief amount, the median amount of relief reported was approximately $124. For the approximately 330 consumer loan complaints where companies provided a relief amount, the median amount of relief reported was approximately $214.For the approximately 300 student loan complaints where companies provided a relief amount, the median amount of relief reported was approximately $170. For the approximately 150 money transfer complaints where companies provided a relief amount, the median amount of relief reported was approximately $127. For the approximately 70 payday loan complaints where companies provided a relief amount, the median amount of relief reported was approximately $300. Companies rarely report providing monetary relief in response to consumers' debt collection and credit reporting complaints. For the approximately 930 mortgage complaints where companies provided a relief amount, the median amount of relief reported was approximately $460. For the approximately 720 debt collection complaints where companies provided a relief amount, the median amount of relief reported was approximately $346. For the approximately 160 credit reporting complaints where companies provided a relief amount, the median amount of relief reported was approximately $29.

Companies also have the option to provide non-monetary relief in response to complaints. Consumers have received a range of non-monetary relief in response to their complaints, such as:

- providing mortgage foreclosure alternatives that did not include direct monetary payments to the consumer, but that help them to keep their home;

- stopping harassment from debt collectors;

- cleaning up consumers' credit reports by correcting submissions to credit bureaus; restoring or removing a credit line;

- correcting account information, including in credit reports; and

- addressing formerly unmet customer service issues.

## Consumers' reviews of companies' responses

Once the company responds, the CFPB provides the company's response to the consumer for review. Where the company responds "closed with monetary relief," "closed with non-monetary relief," "closed with explanation," or "closed," consumers are given the option to provide feedback on the company's response. Figure 12 shows how consumers responded to the approximately 132,500 complaints where they were given the option to provide feedback.

Consumers are asked to notify the CFPB within 30 days if they want to provide feedback by disputing a company's response. Approximately 65% of such consumers did not dispute the responses provided, while approximately 19% of consumers did dispute the response provided. The rest were pending with consumers at the end of this period.

**FIGURE 12:** CONSUMER FEEDBACK ABOUT COMPANY RESPONSES

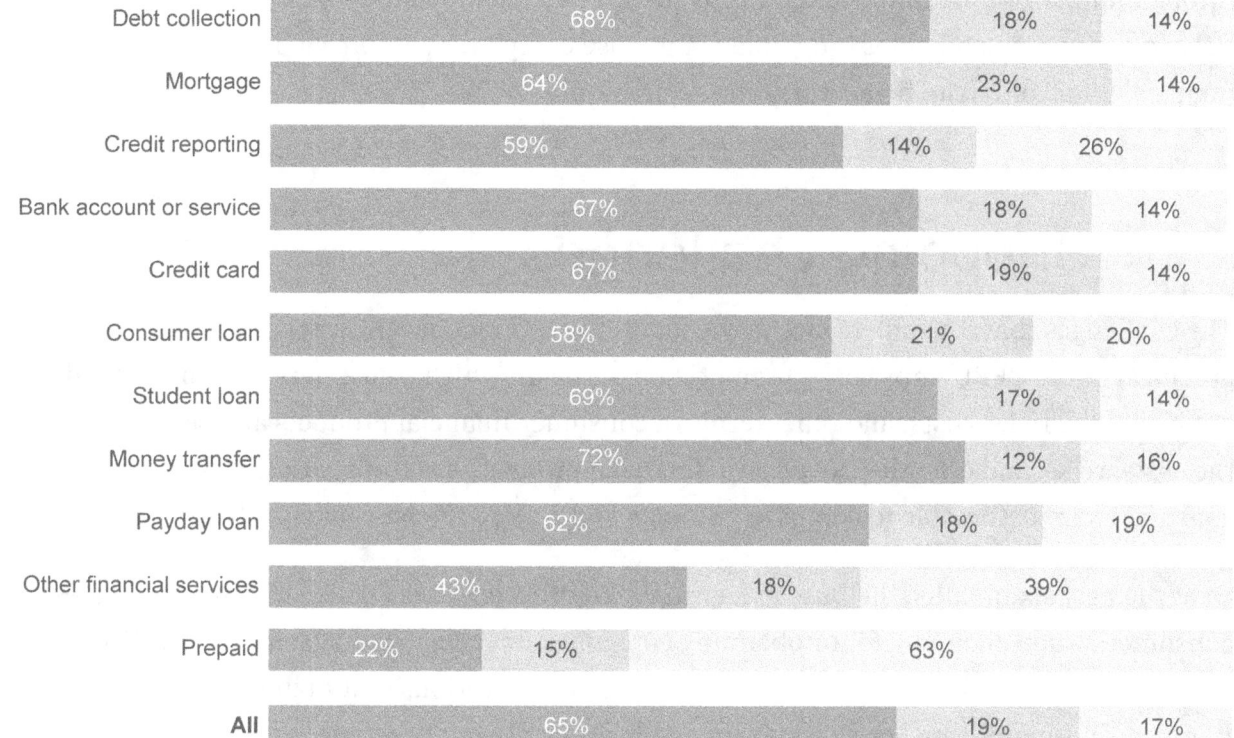

| | | | |
|---|---|---|---|
| Debt collection | 68% | 18% | 14% |
| Mortgage | 64% | 23% | 14% |
| Credit reporting | 59% | 14% | 26% |
| Bank account or service | 67% | 18% | 14% |
| Credit card | 67% | 19% | 14% |
| Consumer loan | 58% | 21% | 20% |
| Student loan | 69% | 17% | 14% |
| Money transfer | 72% | 12% | 16% |
| Payday loan | 62% | 18% | 19% |
| Other financial services | 43% | 18% | 39% |
| Prepaid | 22% | 15% | 63% |
| **All** | 65% | 19% | 17% |

Consumer did not dispute company's response
Consumer disputed company's response
Pending consumer review of company's response

## Consumer response investigation and analysis

After requesting that companies respond to complaints sent to them for response and giving consumers the opportunity to review and provide feedback on company responses, Consumer Response prioritizes complaints for investigation based on a review of the complaint, the company's response, and the consumer's feedback. Consumer Response seeks to determine why a company failed to provide a timely response (if applicable) and whether the consumer's feedback about the company's response (if applicable) justifies additional review of the company's minimum required actions under the consumer financial protection laws within the CFPB's authority. In the course of an investigation, Consumer Response may ask companies and consumers for additional information. In some cases, Consumer Response has referred complaints to colleagues in the CFPB's Division of Supervision, Enforcement, and Fair Lending for further consideration.

Listening to consumers and reviewing and analyzing their complaints is an integral part of the CFPB's work in understanding issues in the consumer financial marketplace, and in helping the market work better for consumers. The information shared by consumers and companies throughout the complaint process informs the Bureau about business practices that may pose risks to consumers and helps the Bureau supervise companies, enforce federal consumer financial laws, and write better rules and regulations.

## 2.2 Shopping challenges

The challenges that consumers face in the marketplace highlight the importance of a tenet that is central to the CFPB's mission – promoting markets in which consumers can understand and anticipate the risks, costs, and other terms of consumer financial products and services. When the costs, risks, and other key features of financial products are transparent and understandable, consumers are better able to compare products and choose the best one for them.

Over the past six months, the Bureau has analyzed different areas that may pose challenges to consumers when shopping for or obtaining consumer financial products or services. The following describes our findings from select Bureau publications that highlight challenges in the mortgage closing process, credit reporting with respect to medical debt, and overdraft usage.

### 2.2.1 Mortgage closing

The Dodd-Frank Act required that the CFPB publish a single, integrated disclosure for mortgage loan transactions that combines the documents required under the Truth in Lending Act (TILA) and the Real Estate Settlement Procedures Act (RESPA). In November 2013, the CFPB released the Loan Estimate and Closing Disclosure forms, which will allow the consumer to better compare the final terms and costs of the loan to the terms and costs he or she received in the estimate. The new changes will also help to highlight the most important information, warn the consumer of dangerous products, and limit the types of costs that can increase from the original estimate.[28] These disclosures will take effect in August 2015.

---

[28] 78 FR 79730 (December 31, 2013). Disclosures available at:
http://www.consumerfinance.gov/knowbeforeyouowe/#disclosure.

As part of its regulatory implementation efforts, the CFPB has also decided to take a broader look at the mortgage process. In April 2014, the Bureau released results of preliminary research around the current mortgage closing process.[29] Through in-depth interviews, closing package analyses, requests for information, and other methods, the Bureau sought to better understand the challenges different stakeholders face at closing.

A key challenge in the closing process has been the number and complexity of the documents in the closing package, which make consumers feel overwhelmed and like they have little control over the process. The Bureau also found in many cases that consumers do not see the closing package until they arrive at the closing table. This is often too late to digest information, ask questions about fee changes, or correct errors without delaying the closing. Furthermore, consumers often feel alone in the process; some claim that key participants (e.g., loan officers) are difficult to reach and that they do not know who is available to explain the documents and process.

The Bureau found two causes for these challenges. First, the size and complexity of the closing package was attributed to the high number of federal, state, and local regulations requiring disclosures, as well as to documents lenders and investors add as part of their risk management processes. Second, the closing process has a high level of variability due to the number of stakeholders involved and the fact that neither documents nor practices are uniform across transactions; this variability often leads to increased confusion and errors. Factors that contributed to the variability of forms included the state in which the property is located and whether the loan was a Federal Housing Administration or Department of Veterans' Affairs loan.

Reducing the complexity of documents and size of the closing package can potentially improve the mortgage closing process. The CFPB is interested in working collaboratively with government and industry partners to encourage the use of documents that are more streamlined and consumer-friendly. However, the CFPB recognizes that other stakeholders own or regulate the majority of the closing documents.

---

[29] http://files.consumerfinance.gov/f/201404_cfpb_report_mortgage-closings-today.pdf.

One other potential solution that the Bureau has been exploring is electronic closing (or eClosing). Shifting the closing experience toward a process that relies on technology for stakeholders to review and/or sign the documentation electronically creates an opportunity to improve the closing experience for consumers. Moving mortgage closings to an electronic format, will not, in and of itself, resolve all the challenges associated with the closing process. However, the Bureau believes that eClosings, coupled with the Bureau's vision for additional consumer-friendly features within the eClosing process, can reduce complexity and anxiety and facilitate improvements that could greatly alleviate consumer challenges.

Along with the report on the closing process, the Bureau also released guidelines for a pilot project to study eClosings. The pilot project is designed to enable the CFPB to better understand the role that eClosings can play in addressing consumers' and other stakeholders' pain points. In August 2014, the Bureau announced the selection of participants with whom to work to test different eClosing features. The companies participating in the pilot include a mix of technology vendors providing eClosing solutions and creditors that have contracted to close loans using these solutions. As the CFPB continues with this pilot and its other "Know Before You Owe" efforts, it will continue to work collaboratively with all stakeholders, including other regulators, to implement its new rule for mortgage disclosures[30] and improve the mortgage closing experience for consumers.

## 2.2.2  Medical debt and credit scores

Consumers' credit scores are based on information in credit reports compiled by nationwide credit reporting agencies (NCRAs). With respect to medical debt, information about unpaid medical bills is reported to the NCRAs either directly by the medical service provider (e.g., a doctor) or by a third-party debt collection agency that has purchased the debt or been contracted to collect it. The vast majority of medical debt reported to the NCRAs – about 99.4 percent of accounts – is reported by collection agencies.

The use of medical collections in credit scoring models has generated concerns stemming from the unique circumstances under which these debts arise and come to be reported to the NCRAs.

---

[30] Integrated Mortgage Disclosures under the Real Estate Settlement Procedures Act (Regulation X) and the Truth in Lending Act (Regulation Z), http://www.consumerfinance.gov/regulations/integrated-mortgage-disclosures-under-the-real-estate-settlement-procedures-act-regulation-x-and-the-truth-in-lending-act-regulation-z/.

However, consumers may sometimes be unaware that the medical collections exist on their credit reports or believe these are charges their insurance should have paid. Yet, medical collections could potentially affect future applications for credit and prices such consumers pay for credit.

In May 2014, the CFPB conducted analyses on how credit scoring models treat medical debt.[31] First, the Bureau examined whether medical and non-medical collections are equally predictive about the subsequent credit performance of consumers. The results suggest that the predictive power of the different types of collection differ. Consumers with more medical than non-medical collections had observed delinquency rates that were comparable to those of consumers with credit scores about 10 points higher.

Second, the Bureau conducted a similar analysis that evaluates whether paid and unpaid medical collections are equally predictive of consumer delinquency rates. The results suggest that they are not equally predictive. Consumers with more paid than unpaid medical collections had delinquency rates that were comparable to the rates of consumers whose credit scores were 22 points higher. That is, consumers with paid medical collections were less likely to be delinquent than other consumers with the same credit score.

For consumers with lower credit scores, especially those on the brink of what is considered subprime, a 10 to 22-point difference can affect their interest rates and ability to borrow. Over time, the score difference could end up costing a consumer tens of thousands of dollars on large loans like home mortgages.

## 2.2.3 Checking account overdraft

Users of checking accounts sometimes engage in debit transactions in amounts that exceed their accounts' balances. An overdraft occurs if their financial institution chooses to cover such a transaction. Financial institutions will typically charge a fee for an overdraft, although particular overdrafts may avoid a fee depending on the particular circumstances of the transaction and the

---

[31] http://files.consumerfinance.gov/f/201405_cfpb_report_data-point_medical-debt-credit-scores.pdf.

financial institution's policies. Overdraft fees generally do not vary by the size of the transaction or the amount by which the consumer's account balance falls below zero.[32]

As highlighted in previous CFPB publications, overdraft fees and fees for non-sufficient funds (NSF) transactions affect the total cost of using checking accounts.[33] However, determining this cost when shopping for a checking account can be difficult as consumers may not anticipate future financial behavior and how such actions can influence the cost of the account.

In a report released in July 2014, the CFPB further explored consumers' experiences with overdrafts at a number of large banks.[34] Using a representative sample of account-level and transaction-level checking account histories from several large banks,[35] we investigated issues such as average checking account fees, negative balance episodes, and overdraft incidence by transaction type. Key findings in the report with respect to the banks studied include:

- Overdraft and NSF fees constitute the majority of the total checking account fees that consumers incur. For opted-in consumers, overdraft and NSF fees account for about 75 percent of their total checking account fees and average over $250 per year.

- Most overdraft fees are paid by a small fraction of bank customers: eight percent of customers incur 75 percent of all overdraft fees.

- The propensity to overdraft generally declines with account holder age, with 10.7 percent of the 18-25 age group having more than 10 overdrafts per year, but only 2.8 percent of the 62 and over age group falling into this category.

---

[32] Some institutions have *de minimis* policies in which non-sufficient funds (NSF) and overdraft transactions are not assessed fees if the transaction amount or the amount by which the account balance falls below zero dollars is less than a specified threshold. Some institutions also have caps on the number of overdraft fees and NSF fees that will be assessed in a single day. Institutions may also empower employees to waive fees manually on individual judgment or in accordance with institutional guidelines. Additionally, an observed minority of institutions tier NSF and overdraft fees by transaction amount. However, in general, NSF and overdraft fees are fixed for transactions that do not trigger *de minimis* policies.

[33] http://files.consumerfinance.gov/f/201306_cfpb_whitepaper_overdraft-practices.pdf.

[34] http://files.consumerfinance.gov/f/201407_cfpb_report_data-point_overdrafts.pdf.

[35] Neither the account-level nor transaction-level data contain any directly identifying personal information.

- The number of overdraft transactions and fees varies substantially with opt-in status.[36] Opted-in accounts are three times as likely to have more than 10 overdrafts per year as accounts that are not opted in. Opted-in accounts have seven times as many overdrafts that result in fees as accounts that are not opted in. Disentangling the causal nature of the relationship between opt-in status and overdrafting would require further analysis.

- Transactions that lead to overdrafts are often quite small. In the case of debit card transactions, the median amount that leads to an overdraft is $24 and the median amount of a transaction that leads to an overdraft fee for all types of debits is $50.

- Most consumers who overdraft bring their accounts positive quickly, with more than half becoming positive within with three days and 76 percent within one week.

The Bureau's analysis of the overdraft data is ongoing as the Bureau seeks to gain further insight into some of the questions posed by the white paper the Bureau issued last year.

---

[36] "Opt-in status" refers to the 2009 Federal Reserve Board amendment to Regulation E, subsequently recodified by the CFPB that generally requires financial institutions to obtain affirmative consent from account holders to be charged fees for overdraft coverage on automated teller machine and non-recurring point of sale debit card transactions.

# 3. Delivering for American consumers and leveling the playing field

The CFPB exercises its authorities under Federal consumer financial protection laws to administer, implement, and promote compliance with those laws. To this end, the Bureau has worked to expand the resources it makes available to consumers to build the foundation necessary for making consumer financial markets work better.

## 3.1 Resources for consumers

The CFPB has launched a variety of offices, detailed in each subsection below, to provide assistance and information to consumers. The Bureau strives to provide individualized help to consumers based on their specific issues with financial products and services, and it works to improve financial literacy and capability – among the public as a whole, and among consumers who have experienced particular challenges in the financial markets.

### 3.1.1 Consumer response

As detailed in the previous section, Consumer Response receives complaints and inquiries directly from consumers. The CFPB accepts complaints through its website and by telephone, mail, email, fax, and referral.

Consumers submit complaints on the CFPB website using complaint forms tailored to specific products, and can also log on to the secure consumer portal to check the status of a complaint and review a company's response. While on the website, consumers can chat with a live agent to receive help completing a complaint form. Consumers can also call the Bureau's toll-free number to ask questions, submit a complaint, check the status of a complaint, and more.[37] The CFPB's U.S.-based contact centers handle calls with little-to-no wait times, can provide services to consumers in more than 180 languages, and serve hearing- and speech-impaired consumers via a toll-free telephone number. Cutting-edge technology, including the secure company and consumer portals, makes the process efficient and user-friendly for consumers and companies. The CFPB also provides secure channels for companies to communicate directly with dedicated staff about technical issues.

As Consumer Response processes complaints and responds to inquiries, it continues to seek new ways to improve existing processes to make them as efficient, effective, and easy-to-use as possible. Based on feedback from consumers and companies, as well as its own observations, Consumer Response identifies new opportunities to improve its processes and implement changes with each product launch. By applying the lessons learned through previous complaint function rollouts, it has continued to improve its intake process, enhanced communication with companies, and ensured the system's ease-of-use and effectiveness for consumers, while providing services trusted by consumers and companies alike.

## 3.1.2   Consumer education and engagement

The CFPB's Consumer Education and Engagement Division (CEE) is developing and implementing initiatives to educate and empower consumers to make better-informed financial decisions. Improving financial literacy and capability encompasses many short and longer-term efforts, and CEE seeks to engage consumers by providing information and educational tools designed to provide clear and meaningful assistance to consumers when they need it.

---

[37] To find more information about submitting a complaint, please see Appendix A.

### 3.1.3 Financial education

The Bureau's Office of Financial Education (OFE) focuses its efforts on: (1) developing and implementing initiatives to improve consumers' financial literacy and capability, (2) engaging in ongoing outreach efforts to understand the financial education needs of various communities, and (3) managing a research and innovation portfolio to enhance existing approaches to financial education.

OFE has also continued its work on tax-time savings. For the third year, OFE, in consultation with the Internal Revenue Service, encouraged Earned Income Tax Credit (EITC) eligible recipients to save some portion of their EITC refunds as a seed to grow savings. The initiative uses the free tax preparation services offered to low- and moderate-income taxpayers through Volunteer Income Tax Assistance (VITA) sites to reach EITC-eligible individuals and families. In 2013, OFE and Financial Empowerment partnered with three VITA sites to pilot the CFPB's *Ready? Set, Save!* initiative. This initiative was aimed at encouraging EITC-eligible taxpayers to pre-commit to saving a portion of their refund at the time their taxes are being prepared and they first learn the amount of their EITC credit and expected tax refund. Listening sessions with VITA site coordinators and tax preparers from the 2013 pilot revealed common barriers they encountered to discussing savings with clients, which informed the development of 2014 program materials. In 2014 the Offices piloted an expanded *Ready? Set, Save!* campaign in 13 communities around the country, which included approximately 100 VITA sites. The Bureau provided training and materials to approximately 2,000 volunteer tax return preparers who served approximately 75,000 low- and moderate-income taxpayers. Each VITA site received worksheets, checklists, and posters to encourage taxpayers to consider savings. The training was designed to better equip volunteers to have a conversation about saving with taxpayers at the time they learn the amount of their refund and to inform them about various savings options available, including direct deposit into an account and/or purchasing a Series I savings bond.

In July 2013, the Office of Financial Education initiated a community financial education project to promote access to reliable, unbiased financial education and resources through public libraries across the country. Research indicates that libraries are highly trusted as a source of information, and serve consumers effectively in times of economic stress. These factors, along with library presence in local communities across the country, make them natural partners for financial education.

The work commenced in 2013 continues to the present. In order to develop the project, the Bureau identified a diverse group of partner libraries that could help us learn about library capabilities and constraints, as well as the types of programs that would be attractive and realistic for libraries to implement. With input from government agencies, foundations, and trade associations that work with libraries, we identified initial partner libraries based on a combination of factors. These factors included the diversity of the areas and patrons they serve, the library's experience in working with others in their communities, and a consideration of the interest expressed in participating. We selected some libraries that have been innovative in providing financial education programs and some that had not yet offered financial education programs. We also chose libraries that would represent a range of geographic locations and types of communities. The initial partner libraries are the Brooklyn Public Library, New York; Columbus Metropolitan Library, Ohio; Florence County Library System, South Carolina; Fresno County Public Library, California; Georgetown County Library, South Carolina; Menominee Tribal College, Wisconsin; Orange County Library System, Florida; Pelham Public Library, Alabama; and San Francisco Public Library, California.

The Bureau is also partnering with federal agencies and national organizations that have relationships with libraries and local communities, such as the American Library Association, the FINRA Investor Education Foundation, the U.S. Department of Agriculture National Institute of Food and Agriculture, the Institute of Museum and Library Services, the Federal Reserve Bank of Chicago, and the FDIC. We will work together with the libraries to help them develop partnerships in their communities and build on existing programs, resources, and infrastructure to reach consumers in their neighborhoods. Resources for libraries are available at consumerfinance.gov/library-resources/.

Beyond these specific initiatives, OFE has continued to produce and develop a range of educational materials for consumer reference.

OFE has engaged a variety of communities and stakeholders, and continues to reach out to key financial educators and community leaders. OFE communicates directly with consumers through webinars, listening sessions, and large consumer events. OFE's outreach this year has focused on workplace financial education, youth financial education and policies, and identifying approaches to resolve common financial challenges for consumers. OFE held a number of events around the country to assess needs and establish its priorities in these areas. OFE launched a LinkedIn online discussion group for financial education practitioners, which shares information on trends, news, and practices in financial education. Engaging consumers directly on consumer financial education topics always has been, and remains, a priority for OFE.

The Bureau is an active member of the Financial Literacy and Education Commission (Commission). The Director of the CFPB serves as the Vice-Chair of the Commission, which was created with the broad purpose of improving Americans' financial literacy. It has actively worked to make improvements in the financial capability of young people. This focus and the programs of the Commission are intended to help young people start early in learning about money and building sound habits in order to enable them to be successful throughout their lives. This effort is intended to ensure that parents, teachers, community leaders, and others have the knowledge, resources, and tools available to guide young people to start thinking about financial success as early as possible.

Employers, including the federal government, can play an important role in helping people avoid financial distress and in promoting long-term financial well-being. Employers can do this by implementing practices in the workplace that strengthen financial capability, including making it easier for employees to adopt positive saving and investing habits. The Bureau is developing information for employers about workplace financial education, which we will share with other federal agencies, as well as with state and local governments and private sector employers. The Bureau also launched a targeted workplace initiative focused on empowering public service organizations to help their employees tackle their student debt. As part of this initiative, the Bureau developed a toolkit, Employer's Guide to Assisting Employees with Student Loan Repayment. Public service organizations can use the toolkit to help employees learn about their options and work toward qualifying for federal loan repayment benefits available for student debt, including Public Service Loan Forgiveness. The Bureau is asking public service employers to take a pledge to help their employees in this effort. You can find the pledge at consumerfinance.gov/pledge/.

OFE also continues to advance its research and innovation portfolios by working to develop metrics for success in financial education and to test solutions for consumers as they make regular, everyday financial decisions.

In particular, a project to develop metrics for success in financial education for working age and older American consumers was launched in FY 2013. In the past year, the Bureau completed much of the first phase by developing definitions of financial well-being for working-age and older Americans and developing hypotheses regarding the drivers of financial well-being. This work included:

- Background research on how financial well-being is defined and measured in the literature to date, and what is already known about the relationship between financial knowledge, behavior, and well-being;

- In-depth qualitative interviews with consumers, as well as various types of financial professionals, such as financial educators, advisers, planners, coaches, tax preparers, and credit counselors; and

- Consultation with academic and practitioner experts.

This project should allow the CFPB, other government agencies, and those involved in financial education to further identify approaches to improving consumer financial well-being. In addition, by creating and vetting measures for consumer financial knowledge, behavior, and well-being, the project will create a stronger quantitative basis for evaluating financial education policies and programs. More specifically, these metrics should significantly increase the ability of the CFPB, other government agencies, and other financial education providers to select approaches and criteria that make the biggest contributions to improving consumer outcomes.

## 3.1.4 Consumer engagement

The Consumer Engagement Office (CE) develops digital resources, information, and tools to help consumers make better-informed financial decisions. CE works to create an interactive, informative relationship between the CFPB and consumers, and collaborates with offices and divisions across the Bureau on ways to effectively engage the public. CE approaches this mission with user-centered and data-driven approaches to public engagement.

CE continues to improve and build out the Bureau's online presence with innovative, user-focused, approaches to social media and web development. Through research and user testing, CE has been able to tap into the needs and interests of consumers, thus creating opportunities to engage the public in the moments when the Bureau's tools and resources can be most useful to them.

CE also creates scalable platforms that empower American consumers to navigate financial markets. In particular, *Ask CFPB* is an interactive online tool that gives consumers answers to over 1,000 questions about financial products and services, including credit cards, mortgages, student loans, bank accounts, credit reports, payday loans, and debt collection.[38] Since launching in March 2012, *Ask CFPB* has provided clear, authoritative financial information to more than 2,000,000 unique visitors, and currently receives about 300,000 visits per month.

CE has also prioritized making the Bureau's information more accessible in non-English languages, especially Spanish. According to Census data, 37 million people in the U.S. primarily speak Spanish at home. Recognizing that at least some portion of this population could be well served by Spanish language resources, the Bureau launched *CFPB en Español*, a Bureau website that provides Spanish-speaking consumers a central point of access to the Bureau's resources, in Spanish.[39] The website has four major components: a homepage that highlights CFPB services, *Ask CFPB* content in Spanish, a complaints page that highlights the phone number consumers can call to submit a complaint in Spanish, and an "About Us" page that features a Spanish-language video and introductory content about how the CFPB works to protect consumers. The website was created using responsive design, meaning it is optimized for use on both mobile devices and computers in order to better serve all consumers.

## 3.1.5 Servicemember affairs

The Dodd-Frank Act mandated the establishment of an Office of Servicemember Affairs (OSA) to "be responsible for developing and implementing initiatives for service members and their families," including initiatives intended to "educate and empower service members and their families to make better informed decisions regarding consumer financial products and services." OSA works to improve consumer financial protection for servicemembers, veterans, and their families in a number of ways. OSA partners with the Department of Defense and the Department of Veterans Affairs to provide opportunities for servicemembers, veterans, and their families to receive financial education relevant to their needs. OSA monitors complaints submitted by servicemembers, veterans, and their families. OSA coordinates consumer protection efforts among federal and state agencies related to consumer financial products and services offered to, or used by, military families.

---

[38] http://www.consumerfinance.gov/askcfpb.

[39] http://www.consumerfinance.gov/es/.

## Judge Advocate General's Corps training

The Office of Servicemember Affairs' education efforts have included providing subject-matter expertise to the military legal community. Bureau staff have provided instruction on several occasions at The Judge Advocate General's Legal Center and School located in Charlottesville, Virginia. For example, in April 2014, the Office of Servicemember Affairs teamed up with the Offices of Supervision and Enforcement to provide instruction about consumer risk in the payday loan marketplace as part of a legal assistance training course. These efforts help advance OSA's educational reach by leveraging the extensive consumer law mission of the Judge Advocate General's Corps (JAG), and ensuring that JAG legal assistance attorneys have up-to-date information on federal laws and policies affecting servicemembers in the consumer marketplace.

## On-demand training for service providers

We provide on-demand video training for service providers who assist servicemembers and their families worldwide with financial issues.

In 2013, OSA began hosting an ongoing series of virtual Military Financial Educator Forums on consumer financial topics for service providers who deliver financial, educational, or legal counseling to servicemembers and their families worldwide. The goal of these forums is to supply incremental and easily digestible information to those who provide services to servicemembers and their families on current consumer financial topics.

Content highlights from the video forums are also relayed through social media channels to reach those serving the U.S. military across the globe. External social media partnerships with the Department of Defense and the Military Family Learning Network are used to amplify the message delivered by the video trainings to servicemembers stationed overseas.

In January 2014, OSA began making the forums available as on-demand video trainings on the Bureau website at consumerfinance.gov/servicemembers/on-demand-forums-and-tools/. Over 500 service providers have accessed these virtual training tools since their debut. To date, these trainings include issues in debt collection and solutions for servicemembers with troubled mortgages.

## 3.1.6 Older Americans

The Dodd-Frank Act mandated establishment of an Office of Financial Protection for Older Americans (Office for Older Americans). The functions of the Office for Older Americans include "activities designed to facilitate the financial literacy of individuals who have attained the age of 62 years or more . . . on protection from unfair, deceptive, and abusive practices and on current and future financial choices, including through the dissemination of materials to seniors on such topics." More specifically, the statute directs the Office for Older Americans to, among other things, (1) develop goals for financial literacy and counseling programs for seniors, including programs that "help seniors recognize warning signs of unfair, deceptive, or abusive practices" and "protect themselves from such practices," and programs that "provide one-on-one financial counseling on issues including long-term savings and later-life economic security"; and (2) "conduct research to identify best practices and effective methods, tools, technology and strategies to educate and counsel seniors about personal finance management . . .." The statute also directs the Office for Older Americans to work with community organizations and other entities that educate and assist older consumers.

### Elder justice coordinating council

The Bureau serves as a member agency of the Elder Justice Coordinating Council. The Council was established by the Elder Justice Act of 2009 to coordinate activities related to elder abuse, neglect, and exploitation across relevant federal, state, local, and private agencies and entities. The Council is chaired by the Secretary of Health and Human Services (HHS). The Bureau is one of 11 member agencies, in addition to HHS, that HHS has identified for membership based on administering programs related to abuse, neglect, or financial exploitation of older Americans. The Bureau, through its Office for Older Americans, is coordinating and building cooperative plans with its Council partners to address mistreatment of elders. Older Americans' staff members serve on the Elder Justice Interagency Working Group that staffs the Council. The Working Group has developed recommendations and proposed action steps for the Council based on white papers that were submitted by expert witnesses at the Council's inaugural meeting in October 2012. The Council continues to meet twice a year with active participation of the CFPB.

# Interagency guidance on privacy laws and reporting financial abuse of older adults

In 2012, financial institution representatives raised concerns about whether the privacy provisions of the Gramm-Leach-Bliley Act (GLBA) precluded financial institutions from reporting suspected elder financial abuse. The Office for Older Americans, working in coordination with the CFPB's Office for Supervision Policy, developed interagency guidance for financial institutions to clarify the applicability of privacy provisions of GLBA to their reporting of suspected financial exploitation of older adults. Eight federal regulatory agencies with authority to enforce the privacy provisions of GLBA released the guidance on September 24, 2013. The goal of the guidance is to provide financial institutions more certainty about the legality of reporting suspected abuse. This clarity will facilitate financial institutions' timely reporting of suspected abuse so that law enforcement and Adult Protective Services officials can take appropriate protective action.

The Bureau has launched a nationwide outreach campaign to raise awareness about the guidance and about the importance of reporting suspected elder financial exploitation to appropriate local, state, and federal agencies. The outreach events have included calls with industry, Congressional staff, state agencies and regulators, community groups, and aging advocates; speeches to national organizations; webinars; and presentations to federal interagency groups such as working groups of the Financial Literacy and Education Commission and the Elder Justice Coordinating Council.

It appears that the interagency guidance is succeeding in raising awareness of the problem of elder financial exploitation and has influenced activity by financial institutions. For example, following the release of the guidance, the Senior$afe training program for financial institutions in Maine was launched through a collaborative effort between financial institutions and organizations including the Maine Department of Professional and Financial Regulation and the state's Office of Aging and Disability Services– Adult Protective Services.

## Older Americans protection networks

The Office for Older Americans is assisting older American protection networks of state and local governments, elder justice advocates, law enforcement agencies, financial service providers, and other key stakeholders that are working to improve community response to elder financial exploitation. The primary goals of the networks are to increase prevention of, and improve collaboration and response to, elder financial exploitation. The Office for Older Americans staff has been monitoring and participating in network activities such as community education events, and public awareness campaigns and cross-training programs for stakeholders, first responders, advocates, and industry professionals.

To support this effort, Older Americans has launched a project with the Federal Research Division of the Library of Congress to study the activities undertaken by these networks, their outcomes, and best practices. The study will also inform the creation of a replication guide that communities can use to create a network or to enhance existing ones.[40]

## Money Smart for Older Adults

In June 2013, the CFPB and the FDIC released Money Smart for Older Adults (MSOA), an instructor-led curriculum for the FDIC's Money Smart program to provide older consumers and their caregivers with information on preventing and responding to elder financial exploitation. Older Americans and the FDIC have also developed train-the-trainer materials and offer in-person training sessions for national non-profit organizations and others that express interest in becoming Money Smart Alliance partners. Alliance partners can make presentations to community groups on recognizing and preventing elder financial exploitation. The materials include a PowerPoint, Instructor Guide, and Participant Resource Guide. The Participant Resource Guide presents information about different types of fraud, scams, and exploitation that target older persons and provides tips and warning signs on how to prevent losses and report cases. The Participant Resource Guide is available for download at files.consumerfinance.gov/f/201306_cfpb_msoa-participant-guide.pdf or for order at promotions.usa.gov/cfpbpubs.html. Instructor materials are available from the FDIC at fdic.gov/consumers/consumer/moneysmart/olderadult.html.

Since the release of the curriculum in June 2013, more than 2,300 presenters have been trained by the CFPB; and more than 150,000 Participant Resource Guides have been distributed by the CFPB through intermediaries. To increase the reach of this program, the CFPB and FDIC are working on updating the MSOA content and the Spanish translation of the Participant Resource Guide is scheduled to be released in October 2014.

---

[40] files.consumerfinance.gov/f/201304_CFPB_OlderAmericans_Report.pdf.

## 3.1.7 Students

The Dodd-Frank Act directed the Secretary of the Treasury, in consultation with the Bureau's Director, to designate a Private Education Loan Ombudsman within the Bureau "to provide timely assistance to borrowers of private education loans." The Private Education Loan Ombudsman position is held by the Assistant Director of the Office for Students. The Office for Students works to enhance the ability of students and younger consumers to make financial decisions, including monitoring complaints about private student loans, providing information and tools to help students understand the risks from student loans and other financial products, and identifying policy and marketplace issues with special impact on students and younger consumers.

Financial aid offers from colleges and universities often fail to make basic information clear, such as how much of a particular aid offer is made up of loans that need to be paid back and how much comes from grants that do not. The Higher Education Opportunity Act of 2008 required the Secretary of Education to develop a model financial aid offer format to help students and their families make informed decisions about how to finance postsecondary educational expenses. The Bureau partnered with the Department of Education to develop a "Financial Aid Shopping Sheet" to help students and their families make informed decisions about how to finance postsecondary educational expenses. The shared mission to improve the shopping process for potential student borrowers made the Bureau and the Department of Education natural partners in a Know Before You Owe project on student loans.[41]

The Financial Aid Shopping Sheet is a standardized, easy-to-read form of a financial aid award letter that colleges and universities can send to prospective students. The Shopping Sheet is designed to allow college applicants to better understand the debt implications of their college choice and compare the costs of the schools to which they apply.

In April 2012, the President of the United States issued an Executive Order requiring colleges that accept Department of Defense Tuition Assistance Program funds to provide military students with an offer letter based on the principles developed for the Financial Aid Shopping Sheet, in order to provide better information to recipients of military and veteran education

---

[41] http://www.consumerfinance.gov/students/knowbeforeyouowe/.

benefits.[42] The Executive Order also encourages colleges that accept Post-9/11 G.I. Bill benefits to do the same.

As of March 2014, 2,069 colleges and universities, with a combined enrollment of more than 8.8 million students, had voluntarily agreed to adopt the Financial Aid Shopping Sheet.[43]

The Bureau has continued to develop more tools to help consumers make better financial decisions about paying for college and managing student debt. As part of the *Paying for College* suite of tools, the Bureau launched Repay Student Debt, a combined, expanded version of our tools for borrowers in repayment.

In April 2014, the Bureau published a consumer advisory warning consumers that they can avoid defaults following the death or bankruptcy filing of a co-signer by pursuing a co-signer release.[44] The advisory contained sample instructions borrowers or co-signers may use to instruct their student loan servicer to provide information on co-signer release or advise the consumer when they are eligible for co-signer release. The Bureau also published a mid-year update on student loans that describes complaints received related to the practice of placing borrowers in default when a co-signer dies or files for bankruptcy.[45]

## 3.1.8   Financial empowerment

The Dodd-Frank Act mandated that the Bureau include a unit whose functions are to include providing "information, guidance, and technical assistance regarding the offering and provision of consumer financial products or services to traditionally underserved consumers and communities."[46] "Traditionally underserved consumers" include un-banked and under-banked

---

[42] http://www.whitehouse.gov/the-press-office/2012/04/27/executive-order-establishing-principles-excellence-educational-instituti.

[43] http://www2.ed.gov/policy/highered/guid/aid-offer/shopping-sheet-institutions.xls.

[44] http://www.consumerfinance.gov/blog/consumer-advisory-co-signers-can-cause-surprise-defaults-on-your-private-student-loans/.

[45] http://files.consumerfinance.gov/f/201404_cfpb_midyear-report_private-student-loans-2014.pdf.

[46] DFA 1013(b)(2).

consumers.[47] The Office of Financial Empowerment (Empowerment) directs its efforts toward strengthening financial consumer protection and enhancing the financial capability of low-income and other economically vulnerable consumers who comprise the traditionally underserved.

Empowerment is working to integrate financial empowerment strategies into existing public-sector and non-profit programs that assist low-income and other economically vulnerable people who are among the traditionally underserved.

## Financial empowerment toolkit and training

Empowerment has developed and field tested *Your Money, Your Goals*: a financial empowerment toolkit for social services programs. The toolkit provides tools that social service staff can use to incorporate financial capability information into their work with clients and to make referrals to specialized providers. The toolkit includes information that staff can share with clients on topics such as emergency savings; understanding, correcting, and building credit history; managing debt; cash flow budgeting; and identifying financial products to use to pursue various financial and life goals. The toolkit also includes worksheets and other tools individuals can use to strengthen their personal money management skills. For example, tools to help grow skills in financial tasks such as ordering a credit report or understanding and managing debt.

The Bureau field tested the toolkit in fall 2013 by conducting train-the-trainer webinars for 26 social service organizations located across the country. These organizations in turn provided training to 1,400 frontline social service staff from their own and other organizations on how to use the toolkit in their work. The Bureau then gathered feedback that included the extent to which the staff had used the toolkit with their clients and whether the training increased the confidence of the staff in their knowledge of the topics and their ability to help their clients manage their finances.

After receiving input from field-test users of the toolkit, we finalized the text and released it nationally on July 30, 2014. More information is available at consumerfinance.gov/your-money-your-goals/. We plan to conduct webinar trainings that will be available for sign-up through the CFPB website, as well as in-person and webinar trainings within national organizations to equip

---

[47] DFA 1013(b)(1)(F).

them to train their own staff. The Bureau is also developing customized versions of the toolkit to address particular populations or financial capability needs. For example, we developed an abbreviated toolkit focused on credit reporting and debt collection for use by law school-based legal clinics that work with consumers on these issues.

## Foster youth credit reports

The Child and Family Services Improvement and Innovation Act requires that each child age 16 and older in foster care receive annually a free copy of any consumer credit report pertaining to the child until the child is discharged from foster care, and receive assistance in interpreting and resolving any inaccuracies in the report. State and county child welfare agencies are currently working with the national credit reporting agencies to implement these requirements.

The Offices of Financial Empowerment and Financial Education are working with stakeholders at the HHS Children's Bureau, the Federal Trade Commission, and youth advocacy organizations to help streamline the procedures for child welfare agencies to pull credit reports. We are also assisting them to develop capacity to assist foster youth in identifying identity theft, fraud, and errors, and understanding and resolving inaccuracies in the reports. Most recently the Bureau developed tools, including sample letters for ordering credit reports for foster youth and for disputing credit report errors. The tools include tip sheets to provide guidance to caseworkers who are responsible for pulling and cleaning up credit reports for youth in foster care. These tools are available at consumerfinance.gov/blog/how-to-protect-vulnerable-children-from-identity-theft/.

Youth summer employment programs in local communities offer a unique opportunity to reach young people with financial capability education. Youth who may be entering the workforce for the first time can build habits that may last throughout their working lives. In November 2013, Empowerment, along with federal agency partners from the Financial Literacy and Education Commission, convened a roundtable of national and local leaders to discuss current efforts to help youth build financial capability through employment programs. The successful programs represented at the roundtable included three important components: integrating financial education into existing youth employment programs, partnering with employers, and collaborating with financial institutions to improve access to financial services such as transaction accounts. The discussion also revealed many programs that recognize the need to help youth develop financial skills may not have the time, expertise, or resources to do so. Building on these key takeaways, Empowerment developed tools to help communities that want to include financial capability skills in their youth summer employment programs. The Bureau collaborated with several communities to pilot these new tools in summer 2014.

## 3.2   Outreach

In addition to its efforts to engage specific populations, the CFPB has hosted public events across the country to discuss CFPB initiatives and to solicit input about issues related to consumer financial products and services. The public participated in field hearings on mortgage closing, mobile financial services, consumer complaint database, automobile finance, and other consumer finance issues in Washington, DC; New Orleans, LA; El Paso, TX, and Indianapolis, IN.

An audience member participates during the public session at a field hearing in New Orleans, LA.

In conjunction with these field events, Director Cordray and Deputy Director Antonakes held roundtables with community leaders, legal services attorneys, housing counselors, local officials, community banks, credit unions, housing industry participants, and others as part of the CFPB's commitment to engage with the public. The CFPB also hosted a public meeting of its Consumer Advisory Board in Reno, NV on June 18, 2014.

The Bureau has also actively solicited the perspectives of consumer and civil rights groups, including holding roundtables with community-based organizations across the country. Since April 2014, the Bureau's Office of Community Affairs has engaged thousands of community group representatives through more than 150 meetings, briefing calls, and public appearances.

CFPB senior leadership participates in a field hearing on consumer complaints in El Paso, TX.

The Bureau's Office of Financial Institutions and Business Liaison was established in April 2013 to facilitate and coordinate dialogue with all industry participants, and since April 2014, has hosted more than 300 meetings, briefing calls, and public appearances with financial institutions and financial industry trade associations.

Director Cordray and senior CFPB leadership have also delivered several speeches at widely-attended industry and nonprofit conferences.[48] In addition to direct outreach through field events, roundtables, public meetings, speeches, and briefing calls, the CFPB launched Project

---

[48] A list of speeches given in this reporting period by CFPB personnel may be found in Appendix H of this report.

Catalyst to support innovators in creating consumer-friendly financial products and services. The Bureau believes that markets work best when they are open to new ideas, and that the insights and innovations that come from looking at problems and solutions from new angles hold great potential in our efforts to achieve our mission of making the consumer finance market work for all consumers. Project Catalyst is designed to open lines of communication and foster collaborations that promote consumer-friendly innovation.

To these ends, Project Catalyst has continued to develop its outreach efforts and to introduce policy tools. One policy tool is a pilot program in which Bureau subject matter experts work with entrepreneurial companies to better understand what works for consumers and to inform our policy-making in the process. Another policy tool is a trial disclosure program in which the CFPB provides waivers of federal disclosure requirements for successful applicants to allow them to develop and test innovative and consumer-friendly disclosures. More information about Project Catalyst is available on the CFPB's website.[49]

## 3.3  Partnerships

The Bureau has furthered many existing partnerships and formalized several new ones.

To date, the Bureau has signed numerous memoranda of understanding (MOU) with intergovernmental partners, including federal agencies, state financial regulatory entities, state attorneys general, and municipal law enforcement agencies.[50] The Bureau has also actively solicited the perspectives of consumer and civil rights groups.

Senior Bureau leadership has also testified before Congress 52 times since the Bureau opened its doors in 2011, including six occasions between April 1, 2014 and September 30, 2014.[51]

---

[49] http://www.consumerfinance.gov/ProjectCatalyst/.

[50] Information about Bureau MOUs is available at: consumerfinance.gov/newsroom/.

[51] CFPB testimony before Congress may be found in Appendix G of this report. The numbers in this section conform to the reporting period, while the numbers in Appendix G go back a calendar year to conform with the remaining appendices.

### 3.3.1 Office of the Consumer Advisory Board and Councils

The CFPB's Office of the Consumer Advisory Board and Councils is charged with managing the Bureau's advisory groups and serving as the liaison between advisory group members and the Bureau.[52] In addition to its regular engagements with external stakeholders, the Bureau's outreach also includes the:

- Consumer Advisory Board (CAB);

- Community Bank Advisory Council (CBAC);

- Credit Union Advisory Council (CUAC); and

- Academic Research Council (ARC)

Among its responsibilities, the Office of the Consumer Advisory Board and Councils:

- Manages the policies and procedures for the constitution and management of advisory boards and councils;

- Manages the selection process for the Bureau's advisory boards and councils;

- Conducts agenda setting for advisory board and council meetings;

- Regularly facilitates discussions between the Bureau and advisory board/council members; and

- Recommends policy and associated strategies as suggested by advisory boards and councils.

The Consumer Advisory Board and Councils offer vital insight and perspective of financial service providers as the Bureau strives to issue thoughtful, research-based rules.

The Consumer Advisory Board meets at least twice per year. The Credit Union and Community Bank Advisory Councils each meet, on average, twice per year in person and twice per year by conference call. The Academic Research Council meets once annually.

---

[52] http://www.consumerfinance.gov/blog/category/consumer-advisory-board/.

Participants at the Consumer Advisory Board meeting in Reno, NV.

## Role of the Consumer Advisory Board

Section 1014(a) of the Dodd-Frank Act states:

> *The Director shall establish a Consumer Advisory Board to advise and consult with the Bureau in the exercise of its functions under the Federal consumer financial laws, and to provide information on emerging practices in the consumer financial products or services industry, including regional trends, concerns, and other relevant information.*[53]

The Advisory Board and Councils help the Bureau solicit external stakeholder feedback on a range of topics, including consumer engagement, policy development, and research, and from a range of actors, including academics, industry, community members, and advocates. The advisory boards and councils consult on a variety of cross-cutting topics, report on meetings,

---

[53] Dodd-Frank Act, Pub. L. No. 111-203, § 1014(a).

and the CFPB provides minutes and/or summaries of their meetings on the Bureau's website.[54] Members of the Bureau's board and councils serve for limited, specified terms.

## Membership and public nominating process of the Consumer Advisory Board and Councils

Membership to all the Bureau's Advisory bodies is facilitated through a public process whereby members of the public may apply to serve on a board or council. The Bureau will accept applications for these four advisory bodies on a yearly basis. On April 22, 2014 and August 28, 2014, the Bureau announced the newly appointed board and council members.[55] New CAB members will serve a three-year term and new ARC, CBAC and CUAC members will serve two-year terms.

Section 1014(b) of the Dodd-Frank Act states:

*In appointing the members of the Consumer Advisory Board, the Director shall seek to assemble experts in consumer protection, financial services, community development, fair lending and civil rights, and consumer financial products or services and representatives of depository institutions that primarily serve underserved communities, and representatives of communities that have been significantly impacted by higher-priced mortgage loans, and seek representation of the interests of covered persons and consumers, without regard to party affiliation.[56]*

## Meetings of the Consumer Advisory Board and the other Councils

The Bureau has held five meetings of the Advisory Board and Councils during this reporting period:

- Two CAB meetings – June 2014 in Reno, NV and September 2014 in Washington, DC.

---

[54] http://www.consumerfinance.gov/advisory-groups/advisory-groups-meeting-details/.

[55] http://www.consumerfinance.gov/newsroom/cfpb-announces-new-senior-leaders-and-advisory-board-and-council-members/.

[56] Dodd-Frank Act, Pub. L. No. 111-203, § 1014(b).

- One CBAC meeting – June 2014 by conference call.

- One CUAC meeting – June 2014 by conference call.

- One ARC meeting - April 2014 in Washington, DC.

Director Cordray generally provides remarks at CAB meetings, and these are available on our website. A public hearing has always been a part of Consumer Advisory Board meetings that are held in the field. In the June 2014 meeting, the CAB held the meeting of the full Consumer Advisory Board in a public forum. Beginning in the fall of 2014, the Councils will also hold their full advisory council meetings publicly. This transition aims to provide more transparency into the discussions of the CAB and Councils. The public meeting also provides an opportunity for members of the public to hear the information and expertise CAB and Council members to provide information to the Bureau on the financial issues affecting their communities or constituencies.

## Topics covered with our Consumer Advisory Board and the other councils

The March 2014 Credit Union Advisory Council meeting discussed effects of NCUA oversight, including potential impacts on credit unions offering smaller mortgages, such as effects on credit union participation in the mortgage market and credit access for consumers.[57]

Later in March 2014, the Community Bank Advisory Council met and discussed remittances, auto finance, mortgages, and HMDA. The discussions included challenges banks encounter in connection with the HMDA reporting rules.[58]

In April 2014, the Academic Research Council met for the third time since its inception. In this meeting, the ARC discussed the methodological advances around disclosure, measuring costs and benefits of consumer financial protection for consumers and using administrative frames for surveys of borrowers.

---

[57] While this meeting falls outside the timeframe of this report, its content was not included in the previous report, and so is included here for transparency.

[58] See footnote 54.

In June 2014, the CBAC and CUAC met by conference calls to review the recently announced changes to the meeting structure. During these meetings, CUAC and CBAC members also provided feedback about the Bureau's QM/ATR rules, including how member institutions were doing implementing the mortgage rules. During these calls, staff reviewed the small lender guides on consumerfinance.gov with CUAC and CBAC members.

Our June 2014 meeting with the Consumer Advisory Board in Reno was on trends and themes observed in the mortgage market by Board members. Several topics were discussed during the full Board meeting and during Board committee meetings, including Title XIV mortgage rules, pre-acquired account marketing, complaint management, small dollar credit products, the connection between small dollar lending and traditional payment systems, digital currencies, servicemembers, and ECOA/UDAAP.

In September 2014, the Consumer Advisory Board met in Washington, DC. This meeting included new member orientation, discussion of trends and themes in lending circles, student lending technology and access to financial services, among other topics.

For more information about the CAB and the other CFPB advisory bodies, please visit our website.

# 4. Regulations and guidance

In the past six months, the Bureau has issued a number of proposed and final rules that relate to the Dodd-Frank Act, including updating the reporting requirements of HMDA and adjusting the new mortgage and remittance transfer protections. The Bureau is also working on proposed and final rules on various other matters within its authority that would address longstanding consumer protection concerns in a number of consumer financial services markets. In addition, the Bureau is working on follow-up to an earlier Request for Information seeking public comment on potential projects to streamline regulations. The Bureau also continues to be deeply engaged in assisting the mortgage industry with the implementation of Dodd-Frank Act requirements, including the Bureau's rules combining the TILA and RESPA mortgage disclosures, and the Bureau's 2013 mortgage rules.

## 4.1  Implementing statutory protections

The CFPB continues to engage in significant activities designed to implement the Dodd-Frank Act consumer protection provisions. Following the Bureau's issuance of mortgage rules in January 2013[59] and the TILA-RESPA combined rule in November 2013, the Bureau has engaged in activities to support the implementation process for these rules with both industry and consumers. Other statutory implementation efforts have involved issuing additional rules issued

---

[59] In January 2013, the Bureau issued several rules implementing changes made by the Dodd-Frank Act to the laws governing various aspects of the mortgage market, including assessments of consumers' ability to repay their loans, mortgage servicing, loan originator compensation, and other topics. These rules, all of which took effect by January 18, 2014, are now providing significant improvements in the mortgage process that benefit both consumers and the mortgage industry alike through strengthened consumer protections and increased efficiencies. The Bureau's implementation activities for these rules are further discussed in section 4.3.

pursuant to Dodd-Frank mandates. Much of the Bureau's activity continues to be mortgage-related:

- In March 2014, the Bureau, in conjunction with the FRB, FDIC, NCUA, OCC, and FHFA, proposed minimum requirements for Appraisal Management Companies as required by the Dodd-Frank Act. The proposed rule also implements the requirement in the Dodd-Frank Act for States to report to the Appraisal Subcommittee of the Federal Financial Institutions Examination Council (FFIEC) the information required by the Appraisal Subcommittee to administer the new national registry of appraisal management companies.

- In April 2014, the Bureau proposed amendments to certain mortgage servicing and origination rules issued in 2013 under Dodd-Frank Act amendments to TILA and RESPA. The proposed rule would provide an alternative small servicer definition for nonprofit entities that meet certain requirements, amend the existing exemption from the ability-to-repay rule for nonprofit entities that meet certain requirements, and provide a limited cure mechanism for the points and fees limit that applies to qualified mortgages.

- In July 2014, the Bureau took steps to provide additional guidance to industry on mortgage-related issues involving the January 2013 mortgage rules. First, the Bureau issued an interpretive rule to clarify application of the ability-to-repay rule in situations where a successor seeks to be added as an obligor to an existing mortgage loan. Second, the Bureau issued a Policy Guidance regarding mortgage brokers who seek to become mini-correspondent lenders. Brokers are subject to different requirements than lenders under the Bureau's mortgage rules, and the guidance provides the public with a non-exhaustive list of questions the Bureau may consider in exercising its supervisory and enforcement authority in determining whether a particular entity was acting as a lender or as a broker in a mortgage transaction.

- In August 2014, the Bureau published proposed amendments to Regulation C in the *Federal Register* to require lenders to report new data elements required by Dodd-Frank Act revisions to HMDA. The Bureau is also using the rulemaking as an opportunity to explore ways to modernize and simplify HMDA data collection and reporting, particularly in light of other regulatory and mortgage market initiatives to improve the consistency of data standards and information flows. Prior to issuing the proposed rule, the Bureau, along with the Small Business Administration Office of Advocacy and the

Office of Management and Budget, launched a small business review panel process to gather input on the rulemaking in February 2014. The Bureau published its report on the small business review panel process along with the HMDA proposed rule. The comment period for the proposed rule closes at the end of October, and the Bureau is preparing to review the feedback provided by the public.

- The Bureau is also continuing to research and analyze certain issues from the January 2013 mortgage rulemakings that warrant additional follow up. For example, it is reviewing for possible further rulemaking certain Dodd-Frank Act provisions implemented by the Bureau's rules that modify general requirements for certain small creditors, including those that operate predominantly in "rural or underserved" areas.

In addition to this mortgage-related work, in April 2014, the Bureau continued to implement comprehensive new protections for consumers in remittance transfers to foreign countries as mandated by the Dodd-Frank Act by issuing a proposal seeking comment on whether to extend a temporary statutory exception that allows certain depository institutions to estimate certain disclosure elements. The Bureau finalized the proposal in August 2014, extending the temporary exception from July 2015 to July 21, 2020. The Bureau also finalized several clarifications to the remittance rule, including with respect to the treatment of remittance transfers sent to U.S. Military installations located abroad.

## 4.2 Addressing longstanding consumer protection and regulatory burden concerns in other markets

In addition to work implementing Dodd-Frank Act mandates relating to mortgages and remittance transfers, the Bureau has focused attention on a number of issues in other consumer financial products and services markets. This work includes rulemakings to revise regulations the Bureau inherited from other agencies, as well as research and other preparations for rulemakings to address several longstanding issues regarding prepaid cards, debt collection, payday loans and deposit advance programs, and overdraft features on deposit accounts.

As reflected in its most recent regulatory agenda, the Bureau has begun work on a number of other potential rulemaking projects to address longstanding concerns in other consumer financial services markets. For example:

- The Bureau is developing a proposed rule building on the comments received concerning its earlier advanced notice of proposed rulemaking (ANPR) on general purpose reloadable prepaid cards, which are currently not subject to the same federal protections as debit and payroll cards or checking accounts. In the course of developing the proposed rule, the Bureau engaged in testing of disclosure forms that might be included in such a rule and in March 2014 made some of the model disclosure forms being tested available for public feedback on its website.

- The Bureau continues to analyze comments received in response to an ANPR concerning debt collection issued in November 2013 and is conducting research, analysis, and outreach as appropriate on this topic. Debt collection generates more complaints to the federal government each year than any other consumer financial services market. The Bureau will also be issuing a survey of consumers to learn about their experiences with credit and debt, including debt collection. The survey will provide information related to debt collection on a broad cross-section of consumers that is not available elsewhere.

- The Bureau is in the process of considering what regulations to propose to address issues in the market for small dollar credit that have been identified through the Bureau's research and public engagement. The Bureau anticipates that before it issues a proposed rule, it would convene a Small Business Review Panel with the Office of Management and Budget and the Office of Advocacy in the Small Business Administration, to gather feedback on any potential proposal from small entities.

- The Bureau is considering whether regulations are warranted to address issues that have been identified in connection with bank and credit union overdraft practices. In June 2013, a Bureau report discussed whether the overdraft costs on consumer checking accounts can be anticipated and avoided. In July 2014, the Bureau issued a second report providing additional information about the outcomes of consumers who do and do not opt in to overdraft coverage for ATM and one-time accounts.

The Bureau has also continued to work on defining larger participants in markets for consumer financial services and products. Under Title X of the Dodd-Frank Act, the Bureau is authorized to exercise supervisory authority over larger participants that it defines by rule.

- In September 2014, the Bureau finalized a rule defining larger participants of the international money transfer market. The rule will allow the Bureau to supervise larger nonbank international money transfer providers, effective December 1, 2014.

- In September 2014,[60] the Bureau proposed a rule that would define larger participants in the market for automobile financing. The proposal also would define "financial product or service" under the Dodd-Frank Act to include additional automobile leases, and makes certain technical corrections to existing larger-participant rules. The comment period will close in December 2014, and the Bureau is preparing to review the feedback provided by the public.

With regard to regulations that the CFPB inherited, the Bureau issued a Request for Information in December 2011 seeking comment on opportunities to streamline, modernize, and harmonize regulations that it inherited from other federal agencies. The Bureau has sought to address such issues in the course of its rulemakings, for instance, by using the rulemakings to consolidate mortgage disclosures under TILA and RESPA to clarify or reduce the burden of existing regulations and by exploring opportunities to reduce unwanted regulatory burden as part of the HMDA rulemaking.

The Bureau has also launched other rulemaking and guidance initiatives designed to streamline existing regulations. In May 2014, the Bureau issued a Notice of Proposed Rulemaking to seek comment on ways to provide more efficient delivery of annual notices regarding financial institutions' information sharing practices under the Gramm-Leach-Bliley Act. In responding to the earlier Request for Information on streamlining, a large number of commenters suggested that the delivery of duplicate paper notices year after year results in unwanted paperwork for consumers and unwarranted costs for industry. At the end of the reporting period, the Bureau was anticipating it would soon issue a final rule to address the situation and reduce compliance burden, particularly on small financial institutions, while maintaining consumer protections.

---

[60] While this report covers activity through September 30, 2014, this regulatory proposal was posted on the Bureau's website on September r17, 2014 and appeared in the *Federal Register* on October 8, 2014, outside of the reporting period.

# 4.3 Facilitating implementation of new regulations

As the Bureau has issued regulations to implement Dodd-Frank Act remittance and mortgage requirements, it has focused intently on supporting the implementation process for these rules with both industry and consumers. The Bureau has continued to provide implementation support for the mortgage rules issued under Title XIV of the Dodd-Frank Act, which went into effect by January 18, 2014, including engaging in public outreach, speaking at industry conferences, and providing training to housing counselors on new mortgage servicing rules.

The Bureau finalized the TILA-RESPA Integrated Disclosure rulemaking in November 2013, and is working on a number of initiatives to help facilitate implementation before the August 2015 effective date:

- Guides and sample forms – shortly after the Bureau finalized the TILA-RESPA rule, the Bureau published two plain-language guides and a number of sample completed forms to assist in the implementation and understanding of the new rules.

  - The Bureau's plain-language compliance guide provides an overview and summary of key aspects of the TILA-RESPA rule. The guide is in an FAQ format, making the content more accessible, and serving as a resource to help institutions identify and plan for any necessary changes. This guide is especially helpful to small businesses with limited legal and compliance staff.

  - The Bureau's guide to forms provides detailed, illustrated instructions on completing the new Loan Estimate and Closing Disclosure. In recognizing unique needs created by the rule, the guide also highlights common situations that may arise when completing the Loan Estimate and Closing Disclosure.

  - The Bureau published a number of sample forms, in both English and Spanish, to provide additional support to lenders as they make any necessary changes to their systems.

  - The Bureau also published a sample timeline that illustrates the new disclosure timing requirements for a sample real estate transaction. This timeline is particularly useful to lenders and settlement service providers that need to adjust their business requirements around the new rules.

- Webinars – In conjunction with the Federal Reserve System, the Bureau has conducted a number of webinars on the TILA-RESPA rule. Early webinars provided an overview of the final rule and the new disclosures and addressed basic compliance questions. The Bureau plans to conduct additional webinars to further facilitate implementation and address specific implementation and interpretive questions. The Bureau intends to hold these webinars periodically throughout the implementation period while regularly soliciting feedback and additional questions in the interim to further facilitate compliance.

- Public outreach – Bureau staff has spoken at a number of industry conferences. The Bureau also convened roundtables in July, August, and September 2014 to obtain feedback from industry participants, including technology vendors. Bureau staff continues to engage in extensive outreach to discuss the mortgage rules, identify and address implementation issues as they arise, and provide informal oral guidance in response to interpretive inquiries from a myriad of stakeholders. The Bureau recognizes that non-profits, like housing counselors, also play a significant role in providing consumers with support in the home buying process, and plans to engage with these stakeholders later in the implementation period.

The Bureau has made regulatory implementation materials and aids that support and assist TILA-RESPA regulatory implementation efforts, including compliance guides, sample forms, and webinar recordings, available on a section of its website dedicated to regulatory implementation. This, along with other communications and outreach efforts, facilitates industry access to information on regulatory requirements and developments, particularly for smaller businesses that may have limited legal and compliance staff.[61] Recently, the Bureau redesigned the regulatory implementation page for increased functionality, as well as to accommodate future growth. The Bureau plans to continue developing additional compliance tools and resources to facilitate implementation and compliance with the new rules.

Bureau staff is also working to monitor implementation of the new rules as they take effect, and to prepare broader research efforts to assess the impact of the rules over time. This information

---

[61] http://www.consumerfinance.gov/regulatory-implementation/.

will provide vital feedback to the Bureau both in assessing the need for follow up within the remittances and mortgage markets and in improving its general rulewriting process over time. With respect to the new TILA-RESPA rule, the Bureau has intensified its implementation support and outreach efforts in an effort to ensure that, with under a year remaining until the effective date of the rule, institutions are making any business process, operational, or technological systems changes that may be necessary to comply with requirements of the new rule and generate the new forms.

Finally, one other important initiative launched by the Bureau to support both new and ongoing compliance efforts is the release of its "eRegulations" project, in which the Bureau released a web-based, open source tool that aims to make regulations easier to navigate, read, and understand. eRegulations presents regulation text and commentary in a clear format, and allows users to compare different versions to identify changes. The Bureau began this effort in October 2013 with the online release of Regulation E (including the new remittance transfer rules) with the goals of increased compliance, more efficient supervision, and improved accessibility.[62] The Bureau unveiled Regulation Z in May 2014, which includes recent rule updates. [63]

---

[62] http://www.consumerfinance.gov/eregulations/1005.

[63] http://www.consumerfinance.gov/eregulations/1026.

# 5. Supervision

The CFPB supervises and examines the nation's largest banks and credit unions, and their affiliates, as well as a wide range of nondepository institutions, many of which have never before been subject to routine federal supervision. The CFPB's two supervisory offices, the Offices of Supervision Examinations and Supervision Policy, are tasked with developing and implementing a nationwide supervisory program for depository and nondepository financial institutions. In conducting its supervisory activities, the CFPB focuses on maintaining consistency across markets, industries, charters, and regions, as well as on ensuring efficient and effective examinations and supervisory work.

During the reporting period, the CFPB pursued several initiatives to review and refine internal processes relating to CFPB supervision, including a review of its existing internal examination report review process, and began to implement recommendations arising out of those initiatives. The CFPB continues to follow a risk-based approach to examinations by prioritizing consumer products and markets that pose significant risks to consumers.

# 5.1 Supervisory activities

Since the last Semi-Annual Report was released in May 2014, the CFPB has issued the following public documents:

## Supervisory Highlights

Continuing the CFPB's policy of transparency, Supervision has committed to periodically issuing "Supervisory Highlights." The goal of this publication is to inform both industry and the public about the development of the CFPB's supervisory program, as well as to discuss broad trends in examination findings in key market or product areas.

The fourth edition of Supervisory Highlights, issued in May 2014,[64] reiterated the importance of robust compliance management systems and shared supervisory observations on short-term, small-dollar lending; consumer reporting; debt collection; and fair lending found and addressed during supervision work completed between November 2013 and February 2014. It also provided updates on examination procedures, CFPB guidance, larger participant rulemakings, and public enforcement actions issued during that period that resulted from or were supported by supervision.

The fifth edition of Supervisory Highlights, issued in September 2014,[65] detailed the CFPB's fair lending supervisory activity in the indirect automobile lending market. It also included information about our recent non-public supervisory actions in the indirect auto lending market. Supervisory and enforcement experience suggests that maintaining strong compliance management, imposing caps on discretionary pricing adjustments, and/or adopting non-discretionary dealer compensation models may limit fair lending risk. Innovation and experience may reveal other compliance options.

---

[64] http://www.consumerfinance.gov/reports/supervisory-highlights-spring-2014/.

[65] http://www.consumerfinance.gov/reports/supervisory-highlights-summer-2014/.

# 5.2 Supervisory guidance

## Guidance regarding brokers shifting to "mini-correspondent" model

In July 2014, the CFPB issued policy guidance on supervisory and enforcement considerations relevant to mortgage brokers transitioning to mini-correspondent lenders.[66] The CFPB issued this policy guidance for mortgage industry stakeholders, consumers, and the public to identify questions the CFPB may consider in exercising its supervisory and enforcement authority under the Real Estate Settlement Procedures Act and its implementing Regulation X, and the Truth in Lending Act and its implementing Regulation Z, with respect to transactions involving mini-correspondent lenders.

## Interpretive rule regarding application of Regulation Z's ability-to-repay rule to certain situations involving successors-in-interest

As discussed in section 4, in July of 2014, the CFPB issued an interpretive rule to clarify that the CFPB's Ability-to-Repay Rule incorporates the existing definition of "assumption under Regulation Z."[67] The interpretive rule clarified that where a successor-in-interest (successor) who has previously acquired title to a dwelling agrees to be added as obligor or substituted for the existing obligor on a consumer credit transaction secured by a dwelling, that the creditor's written acknowledgement of the successor as obligor is not subject to the CFPB's Ability-to-Repay Rule, because such a transaction does not constitute an assumption as defined by Regulation Z.

## Compliance bulletin and policy guidance regarding mortgage servicing transfers

In August of 2014, the CFPB issued a compliance bulletin and policy guidance regarding mortgage servicing transfers. The document provides guidance to mortgage servicers regarding

---

[66] http://files.consumerfinance.gov/f/201407_cfpb_guidance_mini-correspondent-lenders.pdf.

[67] http://files.consumerfinance.gov/f/201407_cfpb_bulletin_mortgage-lending-rules_successors.pdf.

compliance with various aspects of the updated servicing rule as applied to the servicing transfer context.[68]

## Bulletin on credit card promotional offers

In August 2014, the CFPB issued a Bulletin to inform credit card issuers of the risk of engaging in deceptive and/or abusive acts and practices in connection with solicitations that offer a promotional APR on a particular transaction over a defined period of time.[69] The CFPB has observed that certain solicitations for such offers do not clearly and prominently convey that a consumer who accepts the offer and continues to use the credit card to make purchases will lose the grace period on the new purchases if the consumer does not pay the entire statement balance, including the amount subject to the promotional APR, by the payment due date.

# 5.3 Coordination and information sharing with state regulators

The CFPB and state regulators coordinate on examinations under a framework for coordination on supervision and enforcement entered into by the CFPB and the Conference of State Bank Supervisors, acting on behalf of state financial regulatory authorities.[70] Examination coordination under the framework may occur where the CFPB and state regulators each have supervisory jurisdiction over particular banks or nondepository entities. The framework is an outgrowth of information sharing MOUs entered into by the CFPB and 62 state financial regulatory authorities in all 50 states, Puerto Rico, the District of Columbia, and Guam. The MOUs provide that state regulators and the CFPB will work together to achieve examination efficiencies and to avoid duplication of time and resources expended. The MOUs also establish safeguards and restrictions on the treatment of any shared information.

---

[68] www.consumerfinance.gov/f/201408_cfpb_bulletin_mortgage-servicing-transfer.pdf.

[69] http://files.consumerfinance.gov/f/201409_cfpb_bulletin_marketing-credit-card-promotional-apr-offers.pdf.

[70] http://files.consumerfinance.gov/f/201305_cfpb_state-supervisory-coordination-framework.pdf.

# 5.4 Reporting on the Truth in Lending Act, the Electronic Fund Transfer Act, and the Credit Card Accountability Responsibility and Disclosure Act

## 5.4.1 Reporting on TILA, EFTA, and the CARD Act

TILA and EFTA require the CFPB to file an annual report to Congress that includes a description of the administration of functions under TILA and EFTA, and an assessment of the extent to which compliance with TILA and EFTA have been achieved. In addition, Section 502(e) of the Credit Card Accountability Responsibility and Disclosure Act of 2009 (CARD Act) requires reporting on supervisory and enforcement activities with respect to compliance by credit card issuers with applicable Federal consumer protection statutes and regulations.

This part of the CFPB's Semi-Annual Report to Congress will provide the information required by TILA, EFTA, and the CARD Act.

First, it describes the CFPB's and other agencies' enforcement efforts and required reimbursements to consumers by supervised institutions, as they relate to TILA, EFTA, their respective implementing regulations, Regulation Z and Regulation E, and the CARD Act. Second, the report provides an assessment of the extent of compliance with the provisions of TILA, EFTA, and their implementing regulations. This TILA, EFTA, and CARD Act report covers the period between January 1, 2013 and December 31, 2013.[71]

---

[71] In order to facilitate reporting on an interagency basis, this TILA, EFTA, and CARD Act report is based on the full calendar year of 2013. This update is delivered annually in the Fall Semi-Annual Report.

## 5.4.2 TILA: public enforcement actions and reimbursements

The purposes of TILA are: (1) to provide a meaningful disclosure of credit terms to enable consumers to compare the various credit terms available in the marketplace more readily and to avoid the uninformed use of credit; and (2) to protect consumers against inaccurate and unfair credit billing and credit card practices. 15 USC § 1601(a).

The enforcement efforts made, and reimbursements required, by all the agencies assigned enforcement authority under TILA are discussed in this section.

The agencies charged with enforcement of TILA under section 15 USC § 1607 include:

- the CFPB;
- the FDIC;
- the OCC;
- the NCUA;
- the FTC;
- the FRB;
- the Farm Credit Administration (FCA);
- the Department of Transportation (DOT); and
- the Grain Inspection, Packers and Stockyards Administration of the Department of Agriculture (GIPSA).

During the reporting period of January 1, 2013 - December 31, 2013, the following agencies reported enforcement actions under TILA, including:[72]

---

[72] The tables and corresponding discussion do not include CARD Act violations.

**TABLE 13:** ENFORCEMENT ACTIONS RELATED TO TILA

| AGENCY | SUMMARY |
|--------|---------|
| CFPB | Ordered a financial institution and an affiliate to refund servicemembers for violations of law, including TILA, for improperly disclosing fees on auto loans. |
| FDIC | Issued one civil money penalty and nine Cease & Desist orders for violations of TILA. |
| OCC | Entered into a formal agreement with a financial institution that included provisions related to fees charged on mortgage loans. |
| DOT | Issued a civil money penalty against an airline and entered into a consent order with it for failing to timely provide ticket refunds. Initiated an enforcement action against a former air taxi operator for failing to timely process refunds for air transportation purchased by credit cards on cancelled flights. |
| FTC | Issued consent agreements with two automobile dealers for deceptive claims in advertisement about the cost and availability of discounts for their vehicles. Obtained final orders against two auto loan modification operations for charging consumers upfront fees on the false promises of reducing consumers' monthly payments and avoiding repossession of their vehicles. |

No other agencies with TILA enforcement authority reported taking any enforcement actions related to TILA during the January 1, 2013 - December 31, 2013 time period.

For TILA and Regulation Z violations found during the January 1, 2013 - December 31, 2013 time period, the CFPB, FRB, FDIC, and NCUA required 19 institutions to reimburse 53,485 consumers approximately $6.8 million. These totals include reimbursements required by the enforcement actions noted in Table 13 as well as non-enforcement actions. They also include reimbursement stemming from a CFPB consent order with an institution for violations of Federal consumer protection laws, including TILA. The consent order required a refund of an estimated $6.5 million to approximately 50,000 customers for improperly disclosing fees on auto loans and misrepresenting the cost and coverage of add-on products financed along with the auto loans.

### 5.4.3 EFTA: public enforcement actions and reimbursements

The purpose of EFTA is to provide a basic framework establishing the rights, liabilities, and responsibilities of participants in electronic fund and remittance transfer systems. 15 USC § 1693(b).

The enforcement efforts made, and reimbursements required, by all the agencies assigned enforcement authority under EFTA are discussed in this section. The CFPB will continue to consider the potential benefits and costs to consumers and financial service providers in evaluating new rules under EFTA. The CFPB will also continue to monitor the market and evaluate the adequacy of consumer protection under EFTA.

The agencies charged with enforcement of EFTA under 15 USC § 1693o include:

- the CFPB;
- the FDIC;
- the OCC;
- the NCUA;
- the FTC;
- the DOT; and
- the Securities and Exchange Commission (SEC).

During the reporting period of January 1, 2013 - December 31, 2013, the following agencies reported enforcement actions under EFTA, including:

**TABLE 14:** ENFORCEMENT ACTIONS RELATED TO EFTA

| AGENCY | SUMMARY |
|---|---|
| FDIC | Issued seven civil money penalties and seven Cease & Desist orders for violations of EFTA. |
| FTC | Settled a previously filed case involving an individual and four companies that allegedly defrauded consumers with false promises of debt relief and charged them without their consent.<br><br>Obtained a partial summary judgment of charges that a payday lender violated EFTA and Regulation E by requiring consumers' authorization for recurring electronic payments from their bank accounts as a condition of obtaining payday loans. |

No other agencies with EFTA enforcement authority reported taking any enforcement actions related to EFTA during the January 1, 2013 - December 31, 2013 time period.

For EFTA and Regulation E violations found during the same time period, the NCUA required, as a result of non-public enforcement actions, 11 institutions to reimburse 11 consumers a total of $5,800.

## 5.4.4 CARD Act: public enforcement actions and reimbursements

The CARD Act amended TILA to establish fair and transparent practices relating to the extension of credit under an open-end consumer credit plan. Section 502(e) of the CARD Act requires reporting on supervision and enforcement activities undertaken by the Federal banking agencies (the FRB, FDIC, and OCC), and the FTC with respect to compliance by credit card issuers with applicable Federal consumer protection statutes and regulations.

During the reporting period of January 1, 2013 - December 31, 2013, the following agencies reported enforcement actions under applicable Federal consumer protection law:

**TABLE 15:** ENFORCEMENT ACTIONS RELATED TO THE CARD ACT AND RELATED LAWS

| AGENCY | SUMMARY |
| --- | --- |
| OCC | Ordered a financial institution and affiliates to reimburse consumers for illegal credit card practices, including unfair billing practices and deceptive marketing, with respect to credit card "add-on products" such as payment protection and credit monitoring. This enforcement action was taken in conjunction with CFPB and the FDIC.<br><br>Ordered a financial institution and affiliates to reimburse consumers for illegal credit card practices, including unfair billing practices with respect to credit card "add-on products" such as charging consumers for credit monitoring services that they did not receive. This enforcement action was taken in conjunction with the CFPB. |
| FDIC | Issued 16 civil money penalties, seven Cease & Desist Orders, and eight actions requiring restitution, including an action taken with the OCC (see summary above) and the CFPB that required a financial institution and affiliates to refund consumers for illegal credit card practices. |

No other agencies reported taking any enforcement actions related to the CARD Act and related applicable Federal consumer protection laws during the January 1, 2013 - December 31, 2013 time period.

As a result of the enforcement actions noted in Table 15, the CFPB, FDIC, and OCC required three institutions and affiliates to reimburse more than 3.4 million consumers over $402 million.

## 5.4.5 Assessment of compliance and common violations – TILA and EFTA

The FFIEC agencies reported overall compliance by supervised entities with TILA (including those related to open-end credit) and EFTA, and their respective implementing regulations.[73] However, the agencies reported that more institutions were cited for violations of Regulation Z than Regulation E over the reporting period. This section outlines the most frequently cited violations of Regulation Z and Regulation E reported by the FFIEC agencies for the reporting period.

For the reporting period, the most frequently cited violations of Regulation Z reported by the FFIEC agencies were:[74]

- 12 C.F.R. § 1026.18(d) – On closed-end credit, failure to disclose, or accurately disclose, the finance charge, using that term, or a brief description of the term finance charge.

- 12 C.F.R. § 1026.19(a)(1) – On residential mortgage transactions subject to RESPA, failure to make good faith estimates of the disclosures required by 12 C.F.R. § 1026.18 and to deliver or place them in the mail no later than three business days after receiving the written application.

- 12 C.F.R. § 1026.35(b) – On higher-priced mortgage loans, failure to escrow for property taxes.

For the reporting period, the most frequently cited violations of Regulation E reported by the FFIEC agencies were:

- 12 C.F.R. § 1005.11(c) – Failure to comply with the time limits and the investigation requirements for resolving errors in electronic fund transfers.

---

[73] Other agencies either do not conduct compliance examinations or reported general compliance for the laws under their jurisdiction.

[74] Because the FFIEC agencies use different methods to compile the data, the information presented here supports only general conclusions.

- 12 C.F.R. § 1005.11(d)(1) – Failure to provide an adequate written explanation to the consumer when an investigation determines no error or a different error occurred.

- 12 C.F.R. § 1005.11(d)(2) – Failure to notify the consumer that provisional credit has been reversed and honor payments for five business days when an investigation determines no error or a different error occurred.

## 5.4.6 Outreach related to TILA and EFTA

The FFIEC agencies issue guidance and examination procedures to assist supervised institutions in complying with the requirements of TILA and EFTA and their respective implementing regulations. The agencies also provide guidance to industry members on these topics through participation in conferences and outreach events.

In 2013, the FTC hosted a roundtable to examine unauthorized third-party charges on mobile phone bills, the impact of this practice on consumers, and strategies to protect consumers. Also in 2013, the FTC released videos on payday lending, credit cards (specifically, minimum payments on accounts), and prepaid cards.

# 5.5 Examiner training and commissioning

The CFPB's Supervision Learning & Development (SL&D) team is responsible for training and commissioning the CFPB's field examination staff. The primary vehicle for commissioning will be SL&D's Examiner Commissioning Program (ECP). When complete, the ECP will include six instructor-led, classroom-based courses, as well as formal on-the-job training (OJT) modules, formal learning-transfer measures, a rotation assignment, and a comprehensive commissioning exam and case study. Completed and fully-implemented components of the ECP currently include 32 formal OJT modules and the following instructor-led classroom-based courses: Initial Orientation, Operations and Deposits/Prepaid Products, Lending Principles, Fair Lending Examination Techniques, and Capstone course. An Advanced Communications course is in development and will complete the formal classwork for commissioning. SL&D is targeting late FY14 to release a final ECP Policy and the last quarter of the 2014 calendar year to have all components of the ECP completed and implemented.

Once all parts of the ECP are finished and fully deployed, the two paths to examiner commissioning will be through previous commissioning by another federal regulator (as required by the Dodd-Frank Act), and through successful completion of the ECP, including the comprehensive exam. In the meantime, SL&D is currently operating under an Interim Commissioning Policy (ICP), which allows regional directors to submit executive review nomination memos for highly experienced examiners and field managers. Currently, 145 examiners have CFPB commissions.

## 5.6  Technology

The CFPB continues development of an improved Supervision and Examination System. This system aids the CFPB in supervising and enforcing Federal consumer financial law by utilizing current technology to support the monitoring of bank and nondepository entities, and to collaborate across offices to improve the efficiency of the supervisory process. The development of system functionality is prioritized by business needs.

The CFPB has also begun using a Compliance Tool (the Tool) to assist in conducting examinations of entities subject to CFPB supervision. The Tool provides for secure and standardized data submissions to the CFPB, and supports consistency in the examination process across institutions. The Tool is a software system that collects, validates, and analyzes loan portfolio and deposit account data through an automated system. It enables covered entities to upload data securely and improves the ability of CFPB examiners to conduct risk-based and targeted compliance reviews.

# 6. Enforcement

The CFPB aims to enforce the consumer protection laws within the Bureau's jurisdiction consistently and to support consumer-protection efforts nationwide by investigating potential violations both independently and in conjunction with other federal and state law enforcement agencies.

## 6.1 Conducting investigations

Since the CFPB's launch, the Offices of Enforcement and Fair Lending and Equal Opportunity (Fair Lending) have been investigating potential violations of federal consumer financial laws. Some investigations were transferred to the Bureau by the prudential regulators and HUD, and the Bureau initiated other investigations based on potentially problematic practices that Bureau staff identified or consumers and others have reported. In utilizing its investigation resources, Enforcement considers many factors, including amount of consumer harm and the significance of the potential law violation. Investigations currently underway span the full breadth of the Bureau's enforcement jurisdiction. Further detail about ongoing investigations will not generally be made public by the Bureau until a public enforcement action is filed.

## 6.2 Enforcement actions

Section 1016(c)(5) of the Dodd-Frank Act requires the Bureau to include in the semi-annual report "a list, with a brief statement of the issues, of the public supervisory and enforcement actions to which the Bureau was a party during the preceding year." The Bureau was a party in 41 public enforcement actions from October 1, 2013 through September 30, 2014, detailed as follows:

***United States et. al. v. SunTrust Mortgage, Inc.*** (D.D.C. No. 1:14-cv-01028-RMC)
(consent order entered September 30, 2014).

The CFPB joined with the Department of Justice (DOJ), Department of Housing and Urban
Development (HUD), and attorneys general in 49 states and the District of Columbia to file a
joint proposed federal court order which required SunTrust Mortgage, Inc., to provide $500
million in loss-mitigation relief to underwater borrowers. The consent order, which was adopted
by the court, required SunTrust to pay $40 million to approximately 48,000 consumers who lost
their homes to foreclosure and $10 million to the federal government to cover losses it caused to
the Federal Housing Administration, Department of Veterans Affairs, and the Rural Housing
Service. The order prohibits unlawful mortgage servicing practices, including robo-signing and
illegal foreclosure practices, which violated the Consumer Financial Protection Act of 2010
(CFPA), and the order required SunTrust to establish additional homeowner protections,
including protections for consumers in bankruptcy. SunTrust was also ordered to pay a $418
million penalty in a parallel mortgage lending filing by DOJ.

***In the Matter of: Lighthouse Title, Inc.*** (File No. 2014-CFPB-0015) (consent order entered
September 30, 2014).

The CFPB ordered Lighthouse Title, Inc. to pay $200,000 in civil money penalties for violating
RESPA. Lighthouse Title violated RESPA by entering marketing services agreements with
various parties with the agreement or understanding that in return those parties would refer
business to Lighthouse. The CFPB ordered Lighthouse Title to terminate any existing marketing
services agreements and prohibited Lighthouse Title from entering any marketing services
agreements for the duration of the consent order.

***In the Matter of: Flagstar Bank, F.S.B.*** (File No. 2014-CFPB-0014) (consent order
entered September 29, 2014).

In the first enforcement action under the 2013 RESPA Mortgage Servicing Final Rule, the CFPB
took action against Flagstar Bank, F.S.B., for violating the Rule and the CFPA in connection with
servicing defaulted loans. Among other violations, the bank took excessive time to process
borrowers' applications for foreclosure relief, failed to tell borrowers when their applications
were incomplete, denied loan modifications to qualified borrowers, illegally delayed finalizing
permanent loan modifications, and misinformed borrowers about their right to appeal the
denial of a loan modification. Under the consent order, Flagstar is prohibited from acquiring
pools of defaulted loans from third parties until it demonstrates it has the ability to comply with

laws that protect consumers. Flagstar is also ordered to pay $27.5 million in redress to victims and $10 million in civil money penalties.

***In the Matter of: U.S. Bank N.A.*** (File No. 2014-CFPB-0013) (consent order entered September 25, 2014).

The CFPB ordered U.S. Bank to refund an estimated $48 million to approximately 420,000 customers and to pay a $5 million civil money penalty for illegal practices related to "add-on" products. The CFPB found that U.S. Bank engaged in unfair billing practices for certain identity protection products that promised to monitor customer credit and alert consumers to potentially fraudulent activity. A vendor for U.S. Bank billed customers for these products prior to having the authorization necessary to perform the credit monitoring and credit report retrieval services. The Bureau worked with the OCC to end these practices and provide relief for consumers.

**Consumer Financial Protection Bureau & the State of Florida v. Harper, et al.** (S.D. Fla. No. 9:14-cv-80931 JIC) (stipulated preliminary injunctions issued September 15, 2014 and September 23, 2014).

This action involves a nationwide mortgage relief scheme that the CFPB, jointly with the Florida Attorney General, alleges took advantage of financially distressed homeowners in violation of Regulation O. Under the name of the Hoffman Law Group, the defendants promised homeowners that, in exchange for an upfront fee, the defendants would include the homeowners as plaintiffs in mass-joinder lawsuits against their lenders and servicers, which would get homeowners mortgage modifications or foreclosure relief. In reality, the defendants rarely, if ever, obtained meaningful mortgage assistance relief for the consumers. The court issued a temporary restraining order on July 16, 2014, halting the defendants' business practices, placing the corporate defendants into receivership, and freezing the defendants' assets. On September 12, 2014, the clerk entered default against the five corporate defendants who had failed to appear in this matter, and the court entered orders adopting the stipulated preliminary injunctions on September 15, 2014 and September 23, 2014, as to the three remaining individual defendants.

**Consumer Financial Protection Bureau v. Corinthian Colleges, et al.** (N.D. Ill. No. 1:14-cv-07194) (complaint filed September 16, 2014).

On September 16, 2014, the CFPB filed a lawsuit against Corinthian Colleges, Inc., one of the largest for-profit, post-secondary education companies, in federal court. The complaint alleges that Corinthian induced students to take private student loans by deceptively describing the job and career prospects of its graduates as well as Corinthian's career services, and by misrepresenting its job placement rates. Corinthian also engaged in aggressive debt collection practices in violation of the CFPA and the Fair Debt Collection Practices Act (FDCPA).

***Consumer Financial Protection Bureau v. Richard F. Moseley, Sr., et al.*** (W.D. Mo. No. 4:14-cv-00789DW) (temporary restraining order issued on September 9, 2014).

The CFPB filed a lawsuit against a confederation of online payday lenders known as the Hydra Group, and its principals, alleging that they use a maze of interrelated entities to make unauthorized and otherwise illegal loans to consumers. The CFPB alleged that the defendants' practices violate the CFPA, TILA, and EFTA. On September 9, 2014, a federal court in Kansas City issued an *ex parte* TRO against the defendants, ordering them to halt lending operations. The court also placed the companies in temporary receivership, granted the appointed receiver and the CFPB immediate access to the defendants' business premises, and froze their assets.

***Consumer Financial Protection Bureau v. Global Client Solutions, LLC, et al.*** (C.D. Cal. No. 2:14-cv-06643-DDP-JPR) (stipulated final judgment and consent order entered on August 27, 2014).

In a complaint filed in federal court, the CFPB charged Global Client Solutions, a payment processor, and its two principals, Robert Merrick and Michael Hendrix, with violating the Telemarketing Sales Rule by helping debt-settlement companies charge consumers illegal upfront fees. The court entered a stipulated final judgment prohibiting Global Client Solutions from helping other companies collect illegal fees from consumers. The defendants will be subject to monitoring by the CFPB and will be required to make reports to the CFPB to ensure their compliance. The defendants will also pay over $6 million in consumer relief in addition to paying a civil money penalty of $1 million.

***In the Matter of: First Investors Financial Services Group, Inc.*** (File No. 2014-CFPB-0012) (consent order entered August 20, 2014).

The CFPB took action against First Investors Financial Services Group, Inc., for knowingly furnishing inaccurate information about consumers to credit reporting agencies. The inaccurate information likely led to errors in consumers' credit records, which could impair their ability to obtain credit. The CFPB found that First Investors' conduct violated the Fair Credit Reporting Act (FCRA) and the CFPA. First Investors was ordered to pay $2.75 million in civil money penalties, and to implement measures to insure the information the company provides to credit reporting agencies is accurate.

**_In the Matter of: USA Discounters, Ltd._** (File No. 2014-CFPB-0011) (consent order entered August 14, 2014).

The CFPB ordered USA Discounters to refund approximately $350,000 to servicemembers for unfair and deceptive practices relating to installment loans for furniture, electronics, and other home goods. USA Discounters charged active duty servicemembers a fee for a company called SCRA Specialists LLC to assist servicemembers in availing themselves of their rights under the Servicemembers Civil Relief Act (SCRA). In fact, SCRA Specialists never actually performed most of the services offered to servicemembers. The consent order requires USA Discounters to cease engaging in this unlawful conduct, to provide full restitution to all consumers who paid the SCRA Specialists fee since 2009, and to pay a $50,000 civil money penalty.

**_In the Matter of: Amerisave Mortgage Corp., et al._** (File No. 2014-CFPB-0010) (consent order entered August 12, 2014).

The CFPB took action against Amerisave, its affiliate Novo Appraisal Management Corporation, and the owner of both companies, Patrick Markert, for engaging in a deceptive bait-and-switch mortgage lending scheme. The CFPB found that Amerisave lured consumers by advertising misleading interest rates, locked them in with costly-up-front fees, failed to honor its advertised rates, and illegally overcharged them for affiliated "third party" services. The order includes permanent injunctive relief, requiring Amerisave to advertise only rates that are actually available to consumers, retain an outside consultant to help fix its advertising practices, and take other actions to prevent future consumer harm. Amerisave paid over $14.8 million in restitution and a $4.5 civil money million. Markert, in his individual capacity, paid an additional $1.5 million civil money penalty.

**_In the Matter of: Colfax Capital Corp., et al._** (File No. 2014-CFPB-0009) (consent order entered July 29, 2014).

The Bureau took action against Colfax Capital and Culver Capital, also collectively known as "Rome Finance," and two of its owners for violating Regulation Z (Truth in Lending) by failing to accurately disclose credit information in financing for consumer goods sold online or near military bases, and the CFPA by servicing and collecting on financing agreements that state laws rendered void or limited the consumer's obligation to repay. Under the consent order, Rome Finance will cease efforts to collect on any of the outstanding finance agreements, and it paid $1 in civil penalties. Additionally, under the order, Rome and two of its principals are permanently banned from consumer lending.

**_Consumer Financial Protection Bureau v. Stephen Lyster Siringoringo, et al._** (C.D. Cal. No. 8:14-cv-01155-JVS-AJW) (complaint filed July 22, 2014).

The CFPB filed a complaint against three individuals and a company who marketed and sold purported mortgage assistance relief services to consumers. Stephen Lyster Siringoringo, Clausen & Cobb Management Company, Inc., Alfred Clausen, and Joshua Cobb allegedly violated Regulation O and the CFPA by charging advance fees for loan modifications, making misrepresentations related to purported modifications, and failing to make required disclosures. The complaint alleges that consumers paid thousands of dollars each in advance fees, but in numerous instances received none of the promised services or relief.

**_Consumer Financial Protection Bureau v. The Mortgage Law Group, LLP, et al._** (W.D. Wis. No. 3:14-cv-00513-JDP) (complaint filed July 22, 2014).

On July 22, 2014, the CFPB filed a lawsuit in federal district court against The Mortgage Law Group, LLP, (d/b/a The Law Firm of Macey, Aleman & Searns), Consumer First Legal Group, LLC, and their principals Thomas G. Macey, Jeffrey J. Aleman, Jason E. Searns and Harold Stafford. The CFPB alleged that the defendants violated Regulation O and the CFPA by charging illegal up-front fees for mortgage assistance-relief services and by engaging in misleading and deceptive practices, including falsely representing to consumers that they would receive mortgage-assistance-relief services through legal representation.

**_Consumer Financial Protection Bureau v. Frederick J. Hanna & Associates, P.C., et al._** (N.D. Ga. No. 1:14-cv-2211-AT) (complaint filed July 14, 2014).

The CFPB filed a lawsuit in federal court against Frederick J. Hanna & Associates, P.C., a debt-collection law firm, and its managing partners, for violating the FDCPA and the CFPA. The complaint alleged that the defendants operated a lawsuit mill, filing hundreds of thousands of debt-collection lawsuits against consumers in Georgia state court. The CFPB alleged that these suits often relied on deceptive affidavits and faulty or unsubstantiated evidence, and were filed without meaningful attorney involvement. The CFPB is seeking compensation for victims, a civil money penalty fine, and an injunction against the company and its partners.

***In the Matter of: ACE Cash Express, Inc.*** (File No. 2014-CFPB-0008) (consent order entered July 10, 2014).

The CFPB took action against payday lender ACE Cash Express, Inc., for violating the CFPA by engaging in several unfair and deceptive debt collection practices, and one abusive practice—leveraging an artificial sense of urgency to induce delinquent borrowers with a demonstrated inability to repay their existing loan to take out a new ACE loan with accompanying fees. The Bureau found that this practice took unreasonable advantage of the inability of consumers to protect their own interest in selecting or using a consumer financial product or service. Under the consent order, ACE is ordered to reform its collection practices and to cease encouraging or suggesting that delinquent borrowers pay off their existing loan and then take out a new loan with ACE. ACE was also ordered to pay $5 million in restitution and $5 million in civil money penalties.

***In the Matter of: Synchrony Bank, f/k/a GE Capital Retail Bank*** (File No. 2014-CFPB-0007) (consent order entered June 19, 2014).

The CFPB ordered Synchrony Bank, formerly known as GE Capital Retail Bank, to provide an estimated $225 million in relief to consumers harmed by illegal and discriminatory credit card practices, including $56 million in refunds to consumers who were subjected to deceptive marketing practices, and $169 million in redress with respect to violations of ECOA for deceptively marketing credit card add-on products. The bank misrepresented the cost of the products, failed to inform some cardholders that they were ineligible for the products' benefits, failed to explain that they were enrolling consumers in an optional fee-based product, and misrepresented the products' availability. The CFPB also ordered Synchrony Bank to pay $3.5 million in civil money penalties. The violations of ECOA are discussed in the Fair Lending Enforcement section of this Report.

***In the Matter of: Stonebridge Title Services, Inc.*** (File No. 2014-CFPB-0006) (consent order entered June 12, 2014).

The CFPB ordered Stonebridge Title Services to pay a civil money penalty of $30,000 for violating Section 8 of RESPA. Stonebridge paid illegal referral commissions to independent salespeople who referred title insurance business to it. Referral commissions are allowed under RESPA if the recipient of the payment is an employee of the company that is paying the referral. Though the salespeople received W-2 tax forms from Stonebridge, the Bureau determined that they were not bona fide employees.

***In the Matter of: JRHBW Realty, Inc., d/b/a RealtySouth; TitleSouth, LLC*** (File No. 2014-CFPB-0005) (consent order entered May 28, 2014).

The CFPB ordered RealtySouth, Alabama's largest real estate brokerage company, and its affiliated title company, TitleSouth, to pay $500,000 in civil money penalties for violating RESPA. RealtySouth used a preprinted purchase contract – which homebuyers use to make an offer on a house – that either explicitly directed or suggested that title and closing work be performed by TitleSouth. The accompanying affiliated business arrangement disclosure contained dense text, including its own marketing claims, that did not properly highlight to consumers that they were not required to use TitleSouth and could shop around for other title and closing companies. This conduct violated Section 8 of RESPA, which prohibits kickbacks, referrals to affiliated entities without appropriate disclosures, and payment of unearned fees in the context of residential real estate transactions.

***In the Matter of: Bank of America, N.A. and FIA Card Services, N.A.*** (File No. 2014-CFPB-0004) (consent order entered April 9, 2014).

The CFPB ordered Bank of America and FIA Card Service to refund an estimated $727 million to approximately 2.9 million customers and to pay a $20 million civil money penalty for illegal practices related to credit card "add-on" products. The CFPB found that Bank of America and FIA Card Services deceptively marketed two credit card payment protection products that allowed customers to request the cancelation of some amount of credit card debt in the event of certain hardships or life events. Bank of America and FIA Card services also engaged in unfair billing practices for certain identity protection credit card products that promised to monitor customer credit and alert consumers to potentially fraudulent activity. Bank of America and FIA Card Services billed consumers for these products prior to having the authorization necessary to perform the credit monitoring and credit report retrieval services. The Bureau worked with the OCC, who first uncovered the unfair billing practices, to end these practices and provide relief for consumers.

***Consumer Financial Protection Bureau v. ITT Educational Services, Inc.***, (S.D. Ind. No. 1:14-cv-292-SEB-TAB) (complaint filed February 26, 2014).

The CFPB filed a lawsuit against ITT Educational Services alleging that the for-profit college chain engaged in unfair and abusive practices against consumers by pushing its students into high-interest, high-fee loans that the students could not afford and did not want, in violation of the CFPA. The complaint also alleged that ITT violated TILA and Regulation Z by failing to disclose finance charges in connection with installment loans given to students upon graduation.

**Consumer Financial Protection Bureau et al. v. Ocwen Financial Corp. and Ocwen Loan Servicing, LLC**, (D.D.C. No. 1:13-cv-02025-RMC) (final consent judgment and order filed February 26, 2014).

The CFPB, along with authorities in 49 states and the District of Columbia, obtained an order from a federal court against the nation's largest nonbank mortgage loan servicer, Ocwen Financial Corporation, and its subsidiary, Ocwen Loan Servicing, addressing Ocwen's misconduct at every stage of the mortgage servicing process. The consent order requires Ocwen to provide $2 billion in principal reduction to underwater borrowers and to refund over $125 million to nearly 185,000 borrowers who have already been foreclosed upon. The order also extends the standards for servicing loans found in the National Mortgage Settlement, as well as several new standards, to all of Ocwen's loans.

**In the Matter of: 1st Alliance Lending, LLC** (File No. 2014-CFPB-0003) (consent order entered February 24, 2014).

1st Alliance, a Connecticut mortgage lender, was ordered to pay $83,000 in civil penalties after self-reporting to the Bureau that it had violated federal law by illegally splitting real estate settlement fees. 1st Alliance had used a hedge fund to refinance troubled mortgages it obtained from mortgage servicers. But when 1st Alliance obtained financing elsewhere, it continued to split origination and loss-mitigation fees with the hedge fund, notwithstanding the fact that the fund was no longer providing any funding or other services to 1st Alliance, in violation of RESPA. 1st Alliance cooperated with the investigation, admitted liability, and provided information that facilitated other enforcement investigations.

**In the Matter of: PHH Corp. et al.** (File No. 2014–CFPB-0002) (notice of charges filed January 29, 2014).

The CFPB initiated an administrative proceeding against PHH Corporation and its affiliates, alleging that they harmed consumers through a mortgage insurance kickback scheme that started as early as 1995. A CFPB investigation showed that when PHH originated mortgages, it referred consumers to mortgage insurers with which it partnered. In exchange for this referral, these insurers purchased "reinsurance" from PHH's subsidiaries. CFPB alleges that PHH took the reinsurance fees as kickbacks, in violation of RESPA, which protects consumers by banning kickbacks that tend to unnecessarily increase the cost of mortgage settlement services. The

CFPB alleges that because of PHH's scheme, PHH received as much as 40 percent of the premiums that consumers paid to insurers and PHH collected hundreds of millions of dollars in kickbacks, while consumers ended up paying excessive mortgage insurance premiums.

***In the Matter of: Fidelity Mortgage Corp. and Mark Figert*** (File No. 2014-CFPB-0001) (consent order entered January 16, 2014).

The CFPB took action against Fidelity Mortgage Corporation, a Missouri mortgage lender, and its former owner and president, Mark Figert, after an investigation revealed that Fidelity had paid kickbacks in the form of inflated office-space rental payments to a bank in exchange for customer referrals in violation of RESPA. Under the consent order, Fidelity and Figert disgorged $27,076 and paid $54,000 in civil penalties.

***Consumer Financial Protection Bureau and United States of America v. National City Bank*** (W.D. Pa. No. 2:13-cv-01817-CB) (final consent judgment and order entered January 9, 2014).

At the request of the CFPB and the DOJ, a federal district court in Pennsylvania ordered National City Bank—now owned by PNC Bank —to pay $35 million in restitution to African-American and Hispanic borrowers who were charged higher prices on mortgage loans than similarly-situated non-Hispanic White borrowers. This matter is discussed in more detail in the Fair Lending Enforcement section of this report.

***In the Matters of: American Express Centurion Bank, et al.*** (File Nos. 2013-CFPB-0011, 0012, 0013) (consent orders entered December 24, 2013).

The CFPB, working with the FDIC and OCC, ordered American Express to refund approximately $59.5 million to more than 335,000 consumers for illegal credit card practices including unfair billing tactics and deceptive marketing of credit card add-on products. Consumers were misled about benefits of payment protection products, the terms and conditions, and the applicability of certain fees. In addition to consumer refunds, the CFPB has ordered American Express to pay $9.6 million in civil money penalties.

***In the Matter of: Ally Financial Inc. and Ally Bank*** (File No. 2013-CFPB-0010) (consent order entered December 19, 2013).

The CFPB, in close coordination with the Department of Justice, ordered Ally Financial Inc. and Ally Bank (collectively, "Ally") to pay $80 million in damages to harmed African-American, Hispanic, and Asian and Pacific Islander borrowers for discriminatory pricing of indirect auto loans. In addition, the CFPB ordered Ally to pay $18 million in civil money penalties and to take corrective action to prevent future discrimination. This matter is discussed in more detail in the Fair Lending Enforcement section of this report.

***Consumer Financial Protection Bureau v. CashCall, Inc., et al.*** (D. Mass. No. 1:13-cv-13167) (complaint filed December 16, 2013).

The CFPB filed a complaint against an online loan servicer, CashCall, Inc., for engaging in unfair, deceptive, and abusive practices, including debiting consumer checking accounts for loans that were void. The complaint seeks injunctive and monetary relief, as well as penalties for CashCall's allegedly collecting on debts that consumers do not owe.

***In the Matter of GE Capital Retail Bank and CareCredit LLC*** (File No. 2013-CFPB-0009) (consent order entered December 10, 2013).

The CFPB ordered GE Capital Retail Bank and its subsidiary CareCredit to refund up to $34.1 million to potentially more than one million consumers for illegal credit card enrollment practices. At doctors' and dentists' offices around the country, consumers were signed up for CareCredit credit cards thought to be interest free but that actually accrued interest that kicked in if the full balance was not paid at the end of a promotional period. The Bureau's investigation uncovered evidence of deceptive enrollment processes, inadequate disclosures, and poor training of the staff in providers' offices who were responsible for explaining benefits to consumers. GE Capital and CareCredit were ordered to create a reimbursement fund, improve consumer disclosures with plain language descriptions and other consumer protection features, and institute mandatory training for staff responsible for enrollment.

***In re: 3D Resorts-Bluegrass, LLC*** (W.D. Ky. Bankruptcy No. 11-41599) (settlement approved November 13, 2013); ***In the Matter of: 3D Resorts-Bluegrass, LLC*** (File No. 2013-CFPB-0002) (consent order entered December 3, 2013).

In the bankruptcy action, the CFPB filed a proof of claim related to potential violations including alleged misrepresentations by a developer/lot seller and others regarding the registration, marketing, and sale of certain lots on a property known as the Green Farm Resort in Grayson and Breckinridge Counties, Kentucky. In the administrative action, the Bureau filed a Notice of Charges against 3D Resorts-Bluegrass alleging a series of violations of the Interstate Land Sales Full Disclosure Act. The bankruptcy court approved a settlement between the parties, and a consent order in the administrative action was entered on December 3, 2013. Under the settlement agreement and consent order, affected consumers will receive meaningful relief, including, depending on the consumer's circumstance: the option of returning the lots in exchange for forgiveness of the outstanding mortgage, or the option of receiving a payment of $4,000 or $1,000. Among other relief, the Bureau received $50,000 to be distributed to harmed consumers to the extent practicable.

**In the Matter of: Cash America International, Inc.** (File No. 2013-CFPB-0008) (consent order entered November 21, 2013).

In this case, the CFPB took its first enforcement action against a payday lender, Cash America International, Inc., for robo-signing court documents related to debt collection lawsuits, illegally overcharging servicemembers in violation of the Military Lending Act, and destroying records in advance of the Bureau's examination. Cash America was required to complete consumer refunds of up to $14 million and pay a $5 million civil money penalty.

**Consumer Financial Protection Bureau v. Castle & Cooke Mortgage, LLC, et al.** (D. Utah No. 2:13-cv-684DAK) (stipulated final judgment and order entered November 12, 2013).

On July 23, 2013, the CFPB filed a complaint in the United States District Court for the District of Utah against Castle & Cooke Mortgage, LLC, and two of its officers, for violating the Loan Originator Compensation rule, record-retention requirements of Regulation Z, and CFPA. The CFPB alleged that the defendants paid bonuses to loan officers who steered consumers into mortgages with higher interest rates. In addition to injunctive relief prohibiting the unlawful practices, the settlement required the defendants to pay, jointly and severally, consumer redress totaling more than $9.2 million – the amount of money that consumers paid that went to unlawful bonuses. The settlement also required defendants to pay, jointly and severally, a $4 million civil money penalty.

**Consumer Financial Protection Bureau v. Republic Mortgage Insurance Co.** (S.D. Fla. No. 1:13-cv-24146-JAL) (final consent judgment and order entered on November 19, 2013).

The CFPB brought an enforcement action against Republic Mortgage Insurance Company (RMIC), after determining that the premiums it had paid for "captive reinsurance" were kickbacks to mortgage lenders prohibited under RESPA. The court entered a consent order against RMIC enjoining it from entering into captive reinsurance agreements for 10 years, assessing penalties totaling $100,000, and imposing compliance and reporting obligations.

**Consumer Financial Protection Bureau v. Borders & Borders, PLC, et al.** (W.D. Ky. No. 3:13-cv-01047-JGH) (complaint filed October 24, 2013).

The CFPB filed a complaint alleging that Borders & Borders, a real estate closing law firm, had set up joint ventures with local real estate and mortgage brokers for the purpose of funneling kickbacks to those brokers in exchange for referrals to Borders & Borders.

***In the Matter of: Washington Federal*** (File No. 2013-CFPB-0005); ***In the Matter of: Mortgage Master, Inc.*** (File No. 2013-CFPB-0006) (consent orders entered October 9, 2013).

After CFPB examinations uncovered significant errors in the mortgage loan data provided by these two entities under HMDA, the Bureau ordered the companies—a bank and a non-bank—to pay civil money penalties, correct and resubmit data required by HMDA, and to develop and implement effective HMDA compliance management systems to prevent future violations. These matters are discussed in more detail in the Fair Lending Enforcement section of this report.

***Consumer Financial Protection Bureau v. Meracord LLC and Linda Remsberg*** (W.D. Wash. No. 3:13-cv-05871-RBL) (stipulated final judgment and consent order entered on October 4, 2013).

At the request of the CFPB, a federal district court in Tacoma, Washington, ordered a leading debt-settlement payment processor, Meracord, LLC, and its CEO and owner, Linda Remsberg, to pay a $1.376 million civil penalty for helping other companies collect millions of dollars in illegal upfront fees from consumers. Meracord and Remsberg are also subject to a lifetime ban from processing payments for debt relief services and mortgage relief services.

***Consumer Financial Protection Bureau v. Morgan Drexen, Inc., et al.*** (C.D. Cal. No. 13-cv-01267) (complaint filed August 20, 2013).

On August 20, 2013, the CFPB filed a lawsuit in federal district court against a Nevada corporation, Morgan Drexen, Inc. (Morgan Drexen), and its President and Chief Executive Officer, Walter Ledda. In the complaint, the CFPB alleged that Morgan Drexen and Ledda have violated the Telemarketing Sales Rule and the Dodd-Frank Act by charging illegal up-front fees for debt-relief services, and falsely representing to consumers that they would become debt free in months if they worked with Morgan Drexen. On October 7, 2014, the parties filed cross-motions for summary judgment. The motions are currently pending before the court.

***Consumer Financial Protection Bureau v. Gordon, et al.*** (C.D. Cal. No. 12-cv-06147) (stipulated judgment and order entered against various defendants on February 1, 2013; order granting the Bureau's motion for summary judgment against other defendants entered June 26, 2013; appeal pending).

This action involved a nationwide mortgage relief scheme in which the CFPB alleged that the defendants took advantage of financially distressed homeowners by promising to help them obtain loan modifications and charging them advance fees ranging from $2,500 to $4,500. On February 1, 2013, the court entered a stipulated final judgment and order for permanent injunction as to defendants Abraham Michael Pessar, Division One Investment and Loan, Inc., and Processing Division, LLC. On June 26, 2013, the court granted summary judgment in favor of the CFPB against defendants Chance Edward Gordon and the Gordon Law Firm, P.C., finding that those defendants violated the Dodd-Frank Act by falsely representing: (1) that consumers would obtain mortgage loan modifications that substantially reduced consumers' mortgage payments or interest rates and that defendants were affiliated with, endorsed by, or approved by the U.S. government, among other things. The Court also found that Gordon violated Regulation O by receiving up-front payments, failing to make required disclosures, wrongly directing consumers not to contact lenders, and misrepresenting material aspects of defendants' services. The court awarded an $11,403,338.63 judgment for disgorgement and restitution against Gordon. Gordon filed a notice of appeal of the court's decision on August 23, 2013.

# 7. Fair lending

As part of its mandate, the CFPB's Office of Fair Lending (Fair Lending) is charged by Congress with "providing oversight and enforcement of Federal laws intended to ensure fair, equitable, and nondiscriminatory access to credit for both individuals and communities" that are enforced by the CFPB, including the Equal Credit Opportunity Act (ECOA) and the Home Mortgage Disclosure Act (HMDA).[75] This part of Fair Lending's mandate is accomplished primarily through fair lending supervision and enforcement work. Interagency coordination[76] and outreach to industry groups and fair lending, civil rights, consumer and community advocates[77] are also important elements of our mandate. In addition, Fair Lending published a recent report to Congress on the efforts of the Bureau and our fulfillment of our fair lending mandate.[78] Published in April 2014, the Fair Lending Report of the Consumer Financial Protection Bureau[79] provides an overview of risk prioritization process; supervision tools; recent public enforcement actions; interagency coordination efforts and reporting; and outreach activities for all market participants. In this Semi-Annual Report update, we focus on highlights from our fair lending supervision and enforcement activities, and continued efforts in interagency coordination and outreach.

---

[75] Dodd-Frank Act, § 1013(c)(2)(A).

[76] Dodd-Frank Act, §1013(c)(2)(B).

[77] Dodd-Frank Act, §1013(c)(2)(C).

[78] Dodd-Frank Act, § 1013(c)(2)(D).

[79] *See* Consumer Financial Protection Bureau, Fair Lending Report of the Consumer Financial Protection Bureau (Apr. 30, 2014), *available at* http://files.consumerfinance.gov/f/201404_cfpb_report_fair-lending.pdf.

# 7.1 Fair lending supervision and enforcement

## 7.1.1 Fair lending supervision

The CFPB's Fair Lending Supervision program assesses compliance with Federal consumer financial laws and regulations at banks and nonbanks over which the Bureau has supervisory authority. Supervision activities range from assessments of the institutions' fair lending compliance management systems to in-depth reviews of products or activities that may pose heightened fair lending risks to consumers. As part of its Fair Lending Supervision program, the Bureau continues to conduct three types of fair lending reviews at Bureau-supervised institutions: ECOA baseline reviews, ECOA targeted reviews, and HMDA reviews.

In conducting reviews, which may be used to examine for any type of fair lending risk in any product line, CFPB examination teams have observed various factors that indicate heightened fair lending risk, including:

- Weak or nonexistent fair lending compliance management systems (CMS);

- Underwriting and pricing policies that consider prohibited bases in a manner that violates ECOA or presents a fair lending risk;

- Discretionary policies without sufficient controls or monitoring to prevent discrimination;

- Inaccurate HMDA data; and

- Noncompliance with Regulation B's adverse action notification requirements.

If the CFPB identifies situations where fair lending compliance is inadequate, it will direct institutions to establish fair lending compliance programs commensurate with the size and complexity of the institution and its lines of business. If fair lending violations have occurred, the CFPB will require remediation and restitution to consumers, and may pursue other appropriate relief.

Because the Bureau's supervisory activity is confidential, the Bureau publishes regular reports on its website called *Supervisory Highlights*. These reports provide information to all market participants on broad market and supervisory trends the Bureau observes. In our Spring 2014 edition[80], we note that CFPB examination teams have observed instances in which financial institutions lack adequate policies and procedures for managing the fair lending risk that may arise when a lender makes exceptions to its established credit standards. This edition also provides information on elements of a strong compliance management system, including: policies and procedures; monitoring and corrective action; training; board and management oversight.

On September 17, 2014, the Bureau published an edition of *Supervisory Highlights* describing the Bureau's fair lending supervisory activity in the indirect auto lending market.[81] In this edition, we describe the Bureau's fair lending supervisory activity so that industry participants can use the information to ensure that their operations remain in compliance with the ECOA and Regulation B. We also note that to avoid risking liability for violations of the ECOA, indirect auto lenders should take proactive steps to mitigate fair lending risk. Supervisory and enforcement experience suggests that maintaining strong compliance management, imposing strict caps on discretionary pricing adjustments, and/or adopting non-discretionary dealer compensation models may limit fair lending risk. The Bureau recognizes that innovation and experience may reveal other compliance options going forward. In *Supervisory Highlights*, we detail the work that our examination teams have done in identifying discrimination in the pricing of auto loans; requiring lenders to establish and maintain strong compliance management to prevent, detect, and remediate future disparities in pricing on prohibited bases; and securing lender commitments to pay approximately $56 million in damages to provide redress to up to 190,000 harmed consumers identified through our supervisory activity. As discussed in the *Supervisory Highlights*, promoting a fair, equitable, and nondiscriminatory auto lending market continues to be a Bureau priority.

---

[80] http://www.consumerfinance.gov/reports/supervisory-highlights-spring-2014/.

[81] http://www.consumerfinance.gov/reports/supervisory-highlights-summer-2014/.

## 7.1.2 Fair lending enforcement[82]

The CFPB has the authority to bring enforcement actions pursuant to HMDA and ECOA. Specifically, the CFPB has the ability to conduct investigations, file administrative complaints, and hold hearings and adjudicate claims through the CFPB's administrative enforcement process. The CFPB also has independent litigating authority and can file cases in federal court alleging violations of fair lending laws under the CFPB's jurisdiction. Like other Federal bank regulators, the CFPB will also refer matters to the DOJ when it has reason to believe that a creditor has engaged in a pattern of lending discrimination. Over the past year, the CFPB announced five fair lending enforcement actions, in the context of credit cards, mortgage lending, auto finance, and HMDA reporting.

### GE Capital, now known as Synchrony Bank

On June 19, 2014, the CFPB, as part of a joint enforcement action with the DOJ, ordered GE Capital, now known as Synchrony Bank, to provide $169 million in relief to about 108,000 borrowers excluded from debt relief offers because of their national origin. The $169 million represents the value of the offer that the consumer did not receive plus interest and indirect damages. If GE Capital had written off or sold their debt, that debt will be forgiven. As part of the CFPB consent order, GE Capital was also required to refund $56 million to approximately 638,000 consumers who were subjected to deceptive marketing practices.

This order represents the federal government's largest credit card discrimination settlement in history. As part of that action, the Bureau found and the DOJ alleged that GE Capital excluded cardholders with Spanish-preferred indicators on their accounts or with mailing addresses in Puerto Rico from two debt collection offers that were provided to other similarly situated cardholders between January 2009 and March 2012.

The Bureau did not assess penalties with respect to the illegal discrimination, based on a number of factors, including that the company self-reported the violation, self-initiated remediation for the harm done to affected consumers, and fully cooperated with the Bureau's

---

[82] Section 1016(c)(5) of the Dodd-Frank Act requires the Bureau to include in the semi-annual report public enforcement actions the Bureau was a party to during the preceding year, which is October 1, 2013 through September 30, 2014, for this report.

investigation, in accordance with the Bureau's *Responsible Business Conduct: Self-Policing, Self-Reporting, Remediation, and Cooperation* bulletin.[83] This bulletin serves to inform market participants that they may proactively self-police for potential violations, promptly self-report to the Bureau when they identify potential violations, quickly and completely remediate the harm resulting from violations, and affirmatively cooperate with any Bureau investigation above and beyond what is required. If a party meaningfully engages in these activities, which this bulletin refers to collectively as "responsible conduct," it may favorably affect the ultimate resolution of a Bureau enforcement investigation.

## PNC Bank, as successor to National City Bank

On December 23, 2013, the CFPB and the DOJ filed a joint complaint against National City Bank for discrimination in mortgage lending, along with a proposed order to settle the complaint. Specifically, the complaint alleged that National City Bank charged higher prices on mortgage loans to creditworthy African-American and Hispanic borrowers than similarly situated non-Hispanic white borrowers between 2002 and 2008. The DOJ also alleged that National City violated the Fair Housing Act, which similarly prohibits discrimination in residential mortgage lending. This action marked the first joint lawsuit brought in federal court by the CFPB and the DOJ to enforce federal fair lending laws.

The consent order filed by the agencies on December 23, 2013 and entered on January 9, 2014 by the U.S. District Court for the Western District of Pennsylvania required National City's successor, PNC Bank, to pay $35 million in restitution to harmed African-American and Hispanic borrowers. The consent order also required PNC to pay to hire a settlement administrator to distribute funds to victims identified by the CFPB and DOJ. On September 16, 2014, the Bureau published a blog post (available in English[84] and Spanish[85]) announcing the selection of a settlement administrator. The post provided information to consumers on contacting the administrator and submitting settlement forms, including eligibility claims.

---

[83] http://files.consumerfinance.gov/f/201306_cfpb_bulletin_responsible-conduct.pdf.

[84] http://www.consumerfinance.gov/blog/national-city-bank-settlement-administrator-will-contact-eligible-borrowers-soon/.

[85] http://www.consumerfinance.gov/blog/el-administrador-de-negociacion-del-national-city-bank-pronto-se-pondra-en-contacto-con-los-prestatarios-elegibles/.

The CFPB and DOJ's joint investigation began in 2011. The agencies alleged that National City Bank's discretionary pricing and compensation policies caused the discriminatory pricing differences. National City gave its loan officers and brokers the discretion to set borrowers' rates and fees. National City then compensated the officers and brokers from extra costs paid by consumers. Over 76,000 African-American and Hispanic borrowers paid higher costs because of this discriminatory pricing and compensation scheme.

## Ally Financial Inc. and Ally Bank

On December 20, 2013, working in close coordination with the DOJ, the CFPB ordered Ally Financial Inc. and Ally Bank (Ally) to pay $80 million in damages to harmed African-American, Hispanic, and Asian and Pacific Islander borrowers and $18 million in penalties to the CFPB. On the same day, the DOJ filed a complaint and consent order in the U.S. District Court for the Eastern District of Michigan setting forth the same relief. The agencies determined that more than 235,000 minority borrowers paid higher interest rates for their auto loans between April 2011 and December 2013 because of Ally's discriminatory pricing system. This settlement represented the federal government's largest auto loan discrimination settlement in history.

Ally, which is an indirect auto lender, sets a risk-based interest rate, or "buy rate," and then allows auto dealers discretion to charge a higher interest rate to the consumer. This is typically called the "markup." Ally then shares some or all of the revenue from that increased interest rate with the dealer. Markups generate compensation for dealers while giving them the discretion to charge consumers different rates regardless of consumer creditworthiness.

The Ally enforcement action resulted from a CFPB examination that began in September 2012 and evaluated Ally's indirect auto lending program for compliance with ECOA, which prohibits creditors from discriminating against loan applicants in credit transactions on the basis of characteristics such as race and national origin. The CFPB and DOJ's coordinated investigation followed the CFPB's examination and concluded that Ally violated ECOA by charging African-American, Hispanic, and Asian and Pacific Islander borrower's higher markups for their auto loans than similarly-situated non-Hispanic white borrowers. The investigation found that these discriminatory pricing differences resulted from Ally giving dealers the ability and incentive to mark up interest rates.

Under the consent order, Ally will pay $80 million in damages to a settlement fund that will go to harmed African-American, Hispanic, and Asian and Pacific Islander borrowers whose auto loans were purchased by Ally between April 2011 and December 2013. Ally will also pay to hire a settlement administrator to distribute funds to victims identified by the CFPB and DOJ. The CFPB will issue a Consumer Advisory once a settlement administrator is named. Ally must also monitor markups to prevent future discrimination or may choose to eliminate markups altogether. Finally, Ally will pay $18 million in penalties to the CFPB's Civil Penalty Fund.

The CFPB provided guidance on fair lending compliance for indirect auto lending in a March 2013 bulletin. The order in Ally demonstrates the type of fair lending risk identified in the CFPB's bulletin, and is part of a larger joint effort between the CFPB and DOJ to address discrimination in the indirect auto lending market.

## Washington Federal and Mortgage Master, Inc.

On October 9, 2013, the CFPB announced two public enforcement actions related to HMDA[86] and its implementing regulation, Regulation C.[87] These enforcement actions addressed violations of HMDA that the CFPB identified during examinations at Washington Federal Bank of Seattle, WA, a federally insured savings and loan association subsidiary of Washington Federal, Inc.; and Mortgage Master, Inc., a large, privately owned mortgage company. The public enforcement actions resulted in an assessment of $34,000 in civil money penalties against Washington Federal, Inc., and $425,000 against Mortgage Master, Inc. The Bureau's Consent Orders also required both institutions to review, correct, and resubmit their respective HMDA data; and develop and implement HMDA compliance management systems.

During this reporting period and pursuant to Section 706(g) of ECOA, the CFPB has also referred 12 matters to the DOJ with regard to:

- Discrimination on the bases of receipt of public assistance income, sex, marital status, age, race and national origin in mortgage lending;

- Discrimination on the bases of race and national origin in auto finance;

- Discrimination of the bases of age and national origin in credit cards; and

---

[86] 12 U.S.C. § 2801-2810.

[87] 12 C.F.R. pt. 1003

- Discrimination on the bases of receipt of public assistance income, age, marital status and sex in student lending.

## 7.2  Interagency fair lending coordination and outreach

### 7.2.1  Interagency coordination

The Bureau's fair lending activity involves close partnerships and coordination among the Bureau's Federal and state regulatory and enforcement partners. Fair Lending continues to lead the Bureau's fair lending interagency coordination and collaboration efforts by working with partners on the Financial Fraud Enforcement Task Force's Non-Discrimination Working Group, the Interagency Task Force on Fair Lending, and the Interagency Working Group on Fair Lending Enforcement.

### 7.2.2  Fair lending outreach, speeches, and presentations

The CFPB is committed to communicating directly with industry and fair lending, civil rights, consumer, and community groups on its policies, compliance expectations, and priorities. Outreach is accomplished through issuance of Interagency Statements, *Supervisory Highlights*, Compliance Bulletins, and blog posts, as well as through the delivery of speeches and presentations addressing fair lending and access to credit matters.

In September 2014, the Bureau hosted an auto finance field hearing in Indianapolis, IN[88] to facilitate a constructive dialogue between senior Bureau staff and a wide range of auto finance market participants, including industry representatives and consumer advocates. The event featured remarks[89] from Director Cordray, as well as testimony from consumer groups, industry

---

[88] http://www.consumerfinance.gov/newsroom/cfpb-proposes-new-federal-oversight-of-nonbank-auto-finance-companies/.

[89] http://www.consumerfinance.gov/newsroom/prepared-remarks-of-cfpb-director-richard-cordray-at-the-auto-finance-field-hearing/.

representatives, and members of the public. In connection with the hearing, the Bureau released a proposed rule to provide more complete Federal oversight of the auto finance market by extending the Bureau's supervision authority to the larger participants in the nonbank auto finance market.[90]  As noted in the Fair Lending Supervision section, the Bureau also released an edition of *Supervisory Highlights* that focused exclusively on indirect auto lending.

In conjunction with the field hearing the Bureau released a white paper[91] on the methodology that the Bureau uses to identify discriminatory practices when self-reported demographic data are unavailable, as well as the accompanying statistical software code.[92] In order to evaluate a lender's compliance with fair lending laws, Bureau examination teams use a proxy methodology just as other Federal supervisory agencies and many private companies do. The white paper, entitled *Using Publicly Available Information to Proxy for Unidentified Race and Ethnicity*, details the methodology the Bureau uses to calculate the probability that an individual is of a specific race and ethnicity based on their last name and place of residence. In connection with the release of the report, the Bureau made available the statistical software code and publicly available census data used to build the proxy to enable lenders to perform the same analysis performed by the Bureau's examination teams. Links to these materials are available on our website.[93] The white paper also reports that our proxy methodology, which combines information on surname and geography, is more accurate than a proxy that relies on either surname or geographic data individually.

CFPB leadership and staff continue to deliver testimony, speeches, panel remarks, and presentations to diverse audiences, including Members of Congress and staff, industry, national and state fair lending and fair housing groups, and community and consumer advocates.

---

[90] Defining Larger Participants of the Automobile Financing Market (proposed Sept. 2014) (to be codified at 12 CFR Parts 1001 and 1090), *available at* http://files.consumerfinance.gov/f/201409_cfpb_proposed-rule_lp-v_auto-financing.pdf.

[91] Using Publicly Available Information to Proxy for Unidentified Race and Ethnicity: A Methodology and Assessment (Summer 2014), *available at* http://www.consumerfinance.gov/reports/using-publicly-available-information-to-proxy-for-unidentified-race-and-ethnicity/.

[92] https://github.com/cfpb/proxy-methodology.

[93] http://www.consumerfinance.gov/reports/using-publicly-available-information-to-proxy-for-unidentified-race-and-ethnicity/.

The Bureau looks forward to continued dialogue with these and other stakeholders on important matters related to fair lending and access to credit.

# 7.3    Home Mortgage Disclosure Act

On August 29, 2014 the Bureau published in the *Federal Register* proposed changes to Regulation C, which implements HMDA, to improve information reported about the residential mortgage market.[94] The rule would shed more light on consumers' access to mortgage credit by updating the reporting requirements of HMDA regulations. The Bureau also aims to simplify the reporting process for financial institutions. The proposal would improve the quality and type of HMDA data as required by the Dodd-Frank Act. The public comment period for the proposed rule will end on October 29, 2014.

---

[94] http://www.gpo.gov/fdsys/pkg/FR-2014-08-29/pdf/2014-18353.pdf.

# 8. Building a great institution: update

The CFPB seeks to promote transparency, accountability, and fairness. Built on these values, the CFPB is better able to make consumer financial markets work for consumers, honest businesses, and the economy.

## 8.1 Open government

The Bureau's mission is to be an agency that helps consumer finance work by making rules more effective, by consistently and fairly enforcing the rules, and by empowering consumers to take more control of their economic lives. A critical part of making financial markets work is ensuring transparency in those markets. The CFPB believes that it should hold itself to that same standard and strives to be a leader by being transparent with respect to its own activities. To accomplish this, the Bureau utilizes its website, consumerfinance.gov, as the primary vehicle to share information on the operations and decisions the CFPB undertakes every day.

Recent information posted on our website that illustrates the Bureau's commitment to openness includes:[95]

- **Organizational Information**

  The CFPB is committed to transparency in a various areas of our organization, including our routine operations. The Bureau maintains a current organization chart in order to show the staff that is responsible at the highest level of management within the Bureau.

- **Procurement Opportunities**

  The Bureau is committed to outlining its future procurement needs by listing a description of the requirement, forecasted solicitation fiscal year, forecasted solicitation quarter, and forecasted acquisition method.

- **Leadership Calendars**

  The CFPB remains steadfast in keeping consumers informed about the daily work of the Bureau's senior leadership by sharing their daily calendars. The Bureau consistently posts the monthly calendars of Director Richard Cordray and Deputy Director Steve Antonakes to its website. The calendars were accessed over 4,500 times during this reporting period. The calendars of past leaders Elizabeth Warren and Raj Date are archived on the Bureau's website for the public to view as well.

- **Budget Updates**

  The CFPB provides a variety of budget documents, financial reports, funding and acknowledgements.[96] The CFPB also provides information related to the Civil Penalty Fund on its website. Information from these items is separated by fiscal year, quarter, and other methods to maintain a higher level of transparency for the public.

---

[95] The open government section of the Bureau's website is consumerfinance.gov/open/, and all documents and pages referenced in this section may be found there.

[96] http://www.consumerfinance.gov/budget/.

- **General Reports**

  The CFPB published its fifth Semi-Annual Report to Congress in May 2014. This report provides Congress and the American people with an update on our mission, activities, accomplishments and publications since our last semi-annual report and contains additional information required by the Dodd-Frank Wall Street Reform and Consumer Protection Act. The CFPB also continues to post a variety of reports to illustrate progress in several areas of the Bureau's operations and activities. Recent reports posted to the CFPB's website include a fair lending report, snapshot of older consumers and mortgage debt, medical debt and credit scores data point, report on the use of remittance histories in credit scoring, a snapshot of consumer complaints received, the 2014 financial literacy annual report, 2014 plain writing compliance report, and the checking account overdraft data point.[97]

- **Guidance Updates**

  The CFPB periodically provides updates on regulations and guidance. The Bureau recently posted an interpretive rule clarifying mortgage lending rules to assist surviving family members[98], guidance regarding brokers shifting to "mini-correspondent" model[99], a compliance bulletin and policy guidance regarding mortgage servicing transfers[100], and interagency guidance regarding unfair or deceptive credit practices.[101]

---

[97] All reports, white papers, and other informational documents are listed in Appendix F, and also may be found at: http://www.consumerfinance.gov/reports/.

[98] http://www.consumerfinance.gov/f/201407_cfpb_bulletin_mortgage-lending-rules_successors.pdf.

[99] http://www.consumerfinance.gov/f/201407_cfpb_guidance_mini-correspondent-lenders.pdf.

[100] http://www.consumerfinance.gov/f/201408_cfpb_bulletin_mortgage-servicing-transfer.pdf.

[101] Jointly with the FRB, FDIC, NCUA, and OCC.
http://www.consumerfinance.gov/f/201408_cfpb_guidance_ffiec_credit-card-practices.pdf.

# 9. Budget

The Bureau is committed to fulfilling its statutory responsibilities and delivering value to American consumers by being accountable and using our resources carefully. The CFPB's Operations Division is responsible for coordinating activities related to the development of the CFPB's annual budget. The Office of the Chief Financial Officer within the Division has primary responsibility for developing the budget, and works in close partnership with the Office of Human Capital, the Office of Procurement, the Technology and Innovation team, and other program offices to develop budget and staffing estimates in consideration of statutory requirements, performance goals, and priorities of the Bureau. The CFPB Director ultimately approves the CFPB budget.

## 9.1 How the CFPB is funded

The CFPB is funded principally by transfers made by the Board of Governors from the combined earnings of the Federal Reserve System, up to the limits set forth in the Dodd-Frank Act. The Director of the CFPB requests transfers from the Federal Reserve System in amounts that he has determined are reasonably necessary to carry out the Bureau's mission. Annual funding from the Federal Reserve System was capped at a fixed percentage of the total 2009 operating expenses of the Federal Reserve System, equal to:

- 10% of these Federal Reserve System expenses (or approximately $498 million) in fiscal year (FY) 2011;

- 11% of these expenses (or approximately $547.8 million) in FY 2012; and

- 12% of these expenses (or approximately $597.6 million) in FY 2013 and each year thereafter, subject to annual adjustments.[102]

The adjusted transfer cap for FY 2014 is $608.4 million. The CFPB had requested transfers from the Federal Reserve totaling $533.8 million to fund CFPB operations and activities for FY 2014.[103] These funds are held in an account for the Bureau at the Federal Reserve Bank of New York.

Bureau funds that are not funding current needs of the CFPB are invested in Treasury securities. Earnings from those investments are also deposited into the Bureau's account.[104]

If the authorized transfers from the Federal Reserve were not sufficient in FY 2010-2014, the CFPB had the authority in those fiscal years to ask Congress for up to $200 million in additional funds, subject to the appropriations process.[105] The CFPB did not request an appropriation in FY 2011, FY 2012, FY 2013 or FY 2014.

## 9.1.1 Fiscal year 2014 spending

In the fiscal year that ended on September 30, 2014, the CFPB incurred approximately $498 million in obligations[106] to carry out the authorities of the Bureau under Federal financial consumer law. Approximately $237 million was spent on employee compensation and benefits for the 1,443 CFPB employees who were on-board by the end of the fiscal year.

In addition to payroll expenses, the largest obligations made through the end of the fiscal year were related to contractual services. Some of the Bureau's significant obligations that occurred in FY 2014 included:

---

[102] *See* Dodd-Frank Act, Pub. L. No. 111-203, Sec. 1017(a)(2).

[103] The Bureau posts all funding request letters on its website at consumerfinance.gov/budget.

[104] *See* Dodd-Frank Act, Pub. L. No. 111-203, Sec. 1017(b).

[105] *See id.* Sec. 1017(e).

[106] An obligation is a transaction or agreement that creates a legal liability and obligates the government to pay for goods and services ordered or received.

- $22.9 million for maintaining ongoing operations of CFPB's consumer contact center and enhancements to the case management database;

- $22.8 million to the Department of Treasury, Departmental Offices for various services such as information technology and human resource systems support;

- $12.1 million to the Department of Treasury, Bureau of Financial Services for cross-servicing of various human resource and financial management services, such as core financial accounting, transaction processing and reporting, travel, and payroll;

- $11.8 million for a one-year building occupancy agreement with the OCC;

- $10.9 million for Bureau-wide IT management and consulting support services;

- $8.2 million to the DOJ for the provision of technical litigation support services and products;

- $7.5 million to the Board of Governors of the Federal Reserve System for Consumer Financial Protection Bureau Office of Inspector General (OIG) for FY 2014 IG services; and

- $6.9 million for supervisory compliance tools that will automate data analysis by providing functionality for examiners to analyze specific loan files in the field.

Table 16 and Table 17 categorize CFPB obligations incurred through the end of FY 2014 by expense category and division/program area:

**TABLE 16:** FY 2014 SPENDING BY EXPENSE CATEGORY

| Expense Category | FY 2014 |
| --- | --- |
| Personnel Compensation | $171,702,000 |
| Benefit Compensation | $65,311,000 |
| Travel | $17,233,000 |
| Transportation of Things | $114,000 |
| Rents, Communications, Utilities & Misc. | $11,050,000 |
| Printing and Reproduction | $2,425,000 |
| Other Contractual Services | $200,031,000 |
| Supplies & Materials | $552,000 |
| Equipment | $21,453,000 |
| Land and Structures | $4,024,000 |
| Interest and Dividends | $0 |
| **Total (as of 9/30/14)** | **$497,895,000** |

**TABLE 17:** FY 2014 SPENDING BY PROGRAM AREA

| Division/Program Area | FY 2014 |
|---|---|
| Office of the Director | $4,185,000 |
| Operations | $112,449,000 |
| Consumer Education & Engagement | $28,438,000 |
| Research, Markets & Regulations | $34,943,000 |
| Supervision, Enforcement, Fair Lending | $135,759,000 |
| Legal Division | $12,424,000 |
| External Affairs | $6,203,000 |
| Other Programs[107] | $2,574,000 |
| Centralized Services[108] | $160,920,000 |
| Total (as of 09/30/14) | $497,895,000 |

As required by the Dodd-Frank Act, the CFPB prepared financial statements for FY 2014. The Government Accountability Office (GAO) rendered an unmodified, or "clean", audit opinion on the CFPB's financial statements. While the GAO did note one material weakness and one significant deficiency in internal controls over financial reporting, the CFPB has already moved forward in taking appropriate steps to implement timely corrective actions and is committed to continuously enhancing and improving its system of internal control. The GAO audit cited no instances of reportable noncompliance with laws and regulations. The CFPB financial

---

[107] Other Programs comprises the costs of the CFPB Office of Ombudsman, Administrative Law Judges, and other CFPB programs.

[108] Centralized services include the cost of certain administrative and operational services provided centrally to other Divisions (e.g., building space, utilities, and IT-related equipment and services).

statements and GAO's opinion are available in the Financial Report of the CFPB for FY 2014 located at http://www.consumerfinance.gov/budget.

## 9.1.2 Civil Penalty Fund

Pursuant to the Dodd-Frank Act, the CFPB is also authorized to collect and retain for specified purposes civil penalties collected from any person in any judicial or administrative action under federal consumer financial laws.[109] The CFPB generally is authorized to use these funds for payments to victims of activities for which civil penalties have been imposed, and may also use the funds for consumer education and financial literacy programs under certain circumstances. The CFPB maintains a separate account for these funds at the Federal Reserve Bank of New York.

### Civil penalty funds collected in Q4, FY 2013[110]

The CFPB reported on civil penalty fund collections for FY 2013, quarters 1, 2 and 3 in CFPB's fifth Semi-Annual Report, dated September 30, 2013. In the fourth quarter of FY 2013, the CFPB collected $20 million in civil penalties from one defendant, JPMorgan Chase.

TABLE 18: TABLE 19: Q4, FY 013 CIVIL PENALTY FUND COLLECTIONS

| Defendant name | CMP collected | Collection date |
| --- | --- | --- |
| JPMorgan Chase | $20,000,000 | October 11, 2013 |
| Total | $20,000,000 | |

### Civil penalty funds collected in FY 2014

In the first quarter of FY 2014, the CFPB collected a total of $37.7 million in civil penalties from 10 defendants. In the second quarter of FY 2014, the CFPB collected a total of $137,000 in civil

---

[109] *See* Dodd-Frank, Pub. L. No. 111-203, Sec. 1017(d).

[110] July 1, 2013 – September 30, 2013

penalties from two defendants. In the third quarter of FY 2014, the CFPB collected a total of $24 million in civil penalties from four defendants. In the fourth quarter of FY 2014, the CFPB collected a total of $30.8 million in civil penalties from eight defendants.[111]

**TABLE 19:** FY 2014 CIVIL PENALTY FUND COLLECTIONS

| Defendant name | CMP collected | Collection date |
|---|---|---|
| Washington Federal | $34,000 | October 11, 2013 |
| Mortgage Master, Inc. | $425,000 | October 15, 2013 |
| Castle & Cooke Mortgage, LLC | $4,000,000 | November 13, 2013 |
| Cash America International, Inc. | $5,000,000 | November 25, 2013 |
| Meracord LLC | $1,376,000[112] | November 26, 2013 July 16, 2014 |
| Republic Mortgage Insurance Company | $100,000 | December 5, 2013 |
| American Express Bank, FSB | $2,000,000 | December 23, 2013 |
| American Express Centurion Bank | $3,600,000 | December 23, 2013 |
| American Express Travel Related Services Company, Inc. | $4,000,000 | December 23, 2013 |
| Ally | $18,000,000 | December 30, 2013 |
| Fidelity Mortgage Corporation | $54,000 | January 21, 2014 |

---

[111] Victims' compensable harm is determined by looking to the terms of the relevant court or administrative order. If the amount of a victim's compensable harm cannot be determined based on the terms of the relevant order, the victim's compensable harm generally will be his or her out-of-pocket losses that resulted from the violation. To determine the amount of a victim's uncompensated harm, the Bureau will take the victim's total compensable harm, and subtract out any compensation that the victim has received—or is reasonably expected to receive—for that harm. *See* 12 C.F.R. § 1075.104.

[112] Meracord agreed to pay $1.376 million in civil penalties in two installments: $555,000 on November 26, 2013 and $821,000 on July 16, 2014.

| | | |
|---|---|---|
| 1<sup>st</sup> Alliance Lending, LLC | $83,000 | March 5, 2014 |
| Bank of America | $20,000,000 | April 17, 2014 |
| RealtySouth | $500,000 | June 4, 2014 |
| Synchrony (GE Capital Retail Bank) | $3,500,000 | June 20, 2014 |
| Stonebridge Title Services, Inc. | $30,000 | June 20, 2014 |
| Ace Cash Express, Inc. | $5,000,000 | June 24, 2014 |
| Colfax (Culver Capital, LLC) | $1 | August 5, 2014 |
| USA Discounters, Ltd. | $50,000 | August 19, 2014 |
| Amerisave Mortgage Corporation | $6,000,000 | August 22, 2014 |
| First Investors Financial Services Group, Inc. | $2,750,000 | August 29, 2014 |
| Global Client Solutions | $1,000,000 | September 5, 2014 |
| **Total** | **$77,502,001** | |

## Civil penalty funds allocated in FY 2014

**Period 2 Allocation: April 1, 2013 – September 30, 2013**

On November 29, 2013, the Bureau made its second allocation from the Civil Penalty Fund. As of September 30, 2013, the Civil Penalty Fund contained an unallocated balance of $56.1 million. This amount was available for allocation pursuant to 12 C.F.R. § 1075.105(c).

**TABLE 20:** PERIOD 2 CASES IN WHICH A CIVIL PENALTY WAS IMPOSED

| Defendant name | Date of final order[113] |
|---|---|
| United Guaranty Corporation | April 8, 2013 |
| Genworth Mortgage Ins. Corp. | April 5, 2013 |
| Mortgage Guaranty Ins. Corp. (MGIC) | April 5, 2013 |
| Radian Guaranty Inc. | April 9, 2013 |
| American Debt Settlement Solutions, Inc. | June 7, 2013 |
| JPMorgan Chase | September 19, 2013 |
| National Legal Help Center[114] | September 23, 2013 |

During Period 2, final orders in Bureau enforcement actions imposed civil penalties in seven cases. The table above lists the date that the order in each of those cases became a "final order" within the meaning of the Civil Penalty Fund rule. Under the Civil Penalty Fund rule, the victims of the violations for which the civil penalties were imposed in these cases are eligible to receive payment from the Civil Penalty Fund to compensate their uncompensated harm.[115]

---

[114] In the National Legal Help Center case, the defendants were ordered to pay $1,050,000 in civil monetary penalties. At the time of this report, the Bureau does not reasonably expect to receive these penalties.

[115] Pursuant to the Civil Penalty Fund Rule, victims' compensable harm is determined by looking to the terms of the relevant court or administrative order. If the amount of a victim's compensable harm cannot be determined based on the terms of the relevant order, the victim's compensable harm generally will be his or her out-of-pocket losses that resulted from the violation. To determine the amount of a victim's uncompensated harm that may be compensated from the Civil Penalty Fund, the Bureau will take the victim's total compensable harm, and subtract out any compensation that the victim has received—or is reasonably expected to receive—for that harm. *See* 12 CFR 1075.104.

Of those seven cases, the Civil Penalty Fund Administrator determined that one case did not have a class of victims with uncompensated harm that is compensable from the Civil Penalty Fund, and that two cases included classes of victims with uncompensated harm that is compensable from the Civil Penalty Fund. As of the time of the allocation, the Fund Administrator was awaiting further information to determine whether classes of victims in the remaining four cases had "compensable harm" or "uncompensated harm" as defined by the Civil Penalty Fund Rule.

The two cases with classes of victims with uncompensated harm that is compensable from the Civil Penalty Fund were American Debt Settlement Solutions, Inc. (ADSS) and National Legal Help Center (NLHC). Specifically, the ADSS victims had $499,248 in uncompensated harm and the NLHC victims had $2.1 million in uncompensated harm.

The Bureau allocated $499,248 to victims in ADSS and $2.1 million to the NLHC class of victims, enough to compensate fully those victim classes' uncompensated harm. No funds were allocated to consumer education and financial literacy programs. The remaining unallocated Civil Penalty Fund balance remained available for future allocations.

TABLE 21: PERIOD 2 ALLOCATION SUMMARY

| Type | Allocation |
|---|---|
| Victim Compensation | $2,557,231 |
| American Debt Settlement Solutions, Inc. | |
| Victim Class Allocation: $499,248 | |
| National Legal Help Center | |
| Victim Class Allocation: $2,057,983 | |
| Consumer Education and Financial Literacy Programs | $0 |
| **Total Allocation** | **$2,557,231** |

**Period 3 Allocation: October 1, 2013 – March 31, 2014**

On May 30, 2014, the Bureau made its third allocation from the Civil Penalty Fund. As of March 31, 2014, the Civil Penalty Fund contained an unallocated balance of $91.4 million. This amount was available for allocation pursuant to 12 C.F.R. § 1075.105(c).

TABLE 22: PERIOD 3 CASES IN WHICH A CIVIL PENALTY WAS IMPOSED

| Defendant name | Date of final order |
| --- | --- |
| Meracord, LLC | October 4, 2013 |
| Washington Federal | October 9, 2013 |
| Mortgage Master, Inc. | October 9, 2013 |
| Castle & Cooke Mortgage, LLC | November 12, 2013 |
| Republic Mortgage Insurance Company | November 19, 2013 |
| Cash America International, Inc. | November 21, 2013 |
| 3D Resorts- Bluegrass, LLC | December 3, 2013 |
| Ally | December 20, 2013 |
| American Express Bank, FSB | December 24, 2013 |
| American Express Centurion Bank | December 24, 2013 |
| American Express Travel Related Services | December 24, 2013 |
| Fidelity Mortgage Corporation | January 16, 2014 |
| 1st Alliance Lending, LLC | February 24, 2014 |

During Period 3, final orders in Bureau enforcement actions imposed civil penalties in thirteen cases. Under the Civil Penalty Fund rule, the victims of the violations for which the civil penalties were imposed in these cases are eligible to receive payment from the Civil Penalty Fund to compensate their uncompensated harm.

Of those cases, the Civil Penalty Fund Administrator determined that two cases did not have eligible classes of victims and seven cases had classes of eligible victims with no uncompensated harm that is compensable from the Civil Penalty Fund. Additionally, as of the time of the Period

3 allocation, the Fund Administrator lacked information to determine whether its classes of victims in one Period 3 case, along with four cases from Period 2, had "compensable harm" or "uncompensated harm" as defined by the Civil Penalty Fund Rule.

Of the three cases that had classes of eligible victims with uncompensated harm, the classes of eligible victims with uncompensated harm in one case are expected to receive full compensation pursuant to an order issued by another federal regulator. The two remaining cases with classes of victims with uncompensated harm that is compensable from the Civil Penalty Fund were Meracord and 3D Resorts-Bluegrass. Specifically, the Meracord victims had $11.5 million in estimated uncompensated harm, and the 3D Resorts-Bluegrass victims had $6.7 million in estimated uncompensated harm. The Bureau allocated $11.5 million to the Meracord victim class and $6.7 million to the 3D Resorts-Bluegrass victim class, enough to compensate fully those victim classes' uncompensated harm. No funds were allocated to consumer education and financial literacy programs. The remaining unallocated Civil Penalty Fund balance is available for future allocation.

TABLE 23: PERIOD 3 ALLOCATION SUMMARY

| Type | Allocation |
|---|---|
| Victim Compensation | $18,246,329 |
| Meracord | |
| Victim Class Allocation: $: $11,542,229 | |
| 3D Resorts- Bluegrass | |
| Victim Class Allocation: $6,704,100 | |
| Consumer Education and Financial Literacy Programs | $0 |
| **Total Allocation** | **$18,246,329** |

Civil penalties collected on or after March 31, 2014 were deposited in the Fund. The amount in the Fund as of September 30, 2014 will be available for allocation following the conclusion of Period 4 in accordance with 12 C.F.R. § 1075.105(c).

## 9.1.3  Bureau-administered redress

Dodd-Frank Act section 1055 authorizes a court in a judicial action, or the CFPB in an administrative proceeding, to grant any appropriate legal or equitable relief for a violation of Federal consumer financial law. Such relief may include redress for victims of the violations, including refunds, restitution, and damages. Relief that is intended to compensate victims is treated as fiduciary funds and deposited into the "Legal or Equitable Relief Fund" established at the Department of the Treasury.

In the first quarter of FY 2014, the Bureau collected $9.2 million in Bureau-Administered Redress funds from Castle and Cooke Mortgage, LLC. Those funds were distributed in the third quarter of FY 2014 to eligible victims in that case in accordance with the terms of the settlement agreement.

In the second quarter of FY 2014, the Bureau collected $50,000 in Bureau-Administered Redress funds from 3D Resorts-Bluegrass, LLC. These funds have not yet been distributed.

The Bureau did not collect any Bureau-Administered Redress funds in the third quarter of FY 2014.

In the fourth quarter of FY 2014, the Bureau collected $14.9 million in Bureau-Administered Redress from Amerisave; $4.0 million in Bureau-Administered Redress from Global Client Solutions; and $27.5 million in Bureau-Administered Redress from Flagstar Bank, F.S.B. These funds have not yet been distributed

# 10. Diversity and excellence

## 10.1 Recruiting and hiring

The CFPB continues a strategic imperative to recruit and hire highly qualified individuals from diverse backgrounds, focusing on filling vacancies at its headquarters in Washington, DC, and in its examiner workforce distributed across the country. The Bureau's examiners are organized by regions and anchored by key strategic satellite offices in three of the nation's financial hubs – Chicago, IL; New York, NY; and San Francisco, CA; and the fourth regional team of examiners is anchored in Washington, DC. As of September 30, 2014, there were 1,443 staff on-board and working to carry out the CFPB's mission.

To meet current and future staffing requirements, the Bureau will continue to evolve its talent acquisition strategies to build a pipeline of talent through the following methods:

### 10.1.1 Becoming an employer of choice

The CFPB recruits inspired, goal-oriented professionals who derive intrinsic value from professional accomplishment. This high-performing workforce supports the CFPB in attracting public-service-minded professionals. The CFPB's brand as an agency that protects consumers directly reinforces the Bureau's brand as an employer. As awareness of the Bureau and its work become prevalent, the image of the CFPB as a great place to work will also be enhanced.

### 10.1.2 Recruit the best from all corners of America

The Bureau is committed to hiring highly-qualified individuals into all positions. In addition to utilizing USA Jobs and the posting of job announcements on the CFPB website, the Bureau achieves its hiring goals through:

- Engaging existing staff and providing them with the tools, messages, and resources to reach out to their own professional networks;

- Leveraging social media to maximize engagement while minimizing cost per applicant;

- External outreach, which includes attendance at professional conferences and university conferences;

- Leveraging the power of numerous digital platforms, including the Professional Diversity Network, to reach diverse talent pools with the competencies necessary to meet the Bureau's needs;

- Enlisting senior leadership to assist with outreach events to attract candidates to the CFPB as a "best place to serve";

- Continuing to utilize professional development programs to build a robust pipeline of talent to meet the current and emerging workforce needs, including the Director's Financial Assistants Program, Pathways Program, and Presidential Management Fellows; and

- Utilizing the Technology and Innovation Fellows Program to find the best and brightest wherever they are, giving them the flexibility to work from wherever they are currently located, attracting talent not usually available to the Federal government.

## 10.1.3 Build a diverse and inclusive workforce

Diversity is a keystone of the Bureau's hiring philosophy. By targeting diverse and specialized candidate pools, the Bureau is able to hire an innovative, professional, and productive workforce that reflects the backgrounds of the consumers we serve. The CFPB participated in dozens of recruiting events at colleges and conferences across the country, of which approximately 40% were primarily focused on diversity hiring initiatives in partnership with the Office of Minority and Women Inclusion (OMWI).

Involving the Bureau's current employees and leaders is also a core component of the Bureau's recruiting strategy. Currently, approximately 250 CFPB staff self-identify as recruiters, sharing and promoting key job opportunities across their respective professional and academic networks.

Additionally, the CFPB partnered with professional groups such as the National Association for Black Accountants and the Association for Latino Professionals in Finance and Accounting to attract qualified candidates for mission-critical occupations at career fairs and expos.

### 10.1.4 Enhance the candidate experience

The CFPB's hiring process has progressed from focusing on immediate, high-impact hiring needs to an integrated, long-term hiring strategy, based on workforce planning best practices.

OHC continues to use tailored assessment methods (e.g., structured interviews, work sample reviews) to support selections for specific positions, and offers training to hiring managers on how to use structured interviews effectively. These candidate assessment strategies continue to enhance the pool of highly-qualified candidates, enable hiring managers to make objective, data-driven employee selection decisions, and build a workforce that demonstrates the key competencies necessary for success at CFPB.

OHC has continued administering its New Employee and Hiring Manager Surveys to identify processes that are working well, as well as areas for improvement.

## 10.2 Staff education, training, and engagement

Since its creation, the CFPB has focused on strong engagement with existing and potential Bureau staff, successfully utilizing education, training, and engagement programs. As the CFPB matures, it has increased both the reach and depth of these programs.

Examples during this reporting period include:

- Offering increased quantity and scope of learning programs for employees and leaders, to include targeted programs for both leaders and individual contributors;

- Continued to make changes to and improve the individual development planning process leveraging an individual development plan template, related developmental guidance, a cross-reference to numerous off-the-shelf learning programs, as well as a career development workshop;

- Continued a project to update and enhance CFPB's competency models, including reviewing proposed work with stakeholders from around the Bureau;

- Conducted a job task and competency analysis for examiner positions to support development of specialized competency-based learning programs and the examiner commissioning program;

- Strengthened a comprehensive coaching program available for the CFPB leadership;

- Conducted an Administrative Conference to provide learning opportunities for administrative staff, to share best practices, and to optimize administrative collaboration;

- Offered 18 Lunch and Learn educational sessions on topics of cross-functional interest which support the CFPB's values of Serve, Lead, and Innovate and which foster successful achievement of our mission;

- Hosted Diversity and Inclusion training events for managers and line-staff along with a number of cultural awareness events to raise awareness and develop cultural competency skills;

- Launched an Effective Feedback Conversations seminar to support positive and constructive performance feedback, set expectations concerning career advancement, and support employee development;

- Developed and delivered internal custom training course for new CFPB supervisors, to cover basic managerial duties as a Federal supervisor or manager;

- Launched internal, custom CFPB Leadership and Management Development series called the Leadership Excellence Seminars, designed to train all supervisors and managers at CFPB on managerial practices and leadership behaviors. Class Sessions are delivered in Cohorts, comprised of a mix of all management levels; Supervisors, Middle Managers, and Executives;

- Developed and delivered internal custom training courses for CFPB team members on Effective Meetings and Effective Teams;

- Partnered with the Office of Students to promote Public Service Loan Forgiveness program;

- Continued *Foundations: Building a Model Financial Workplace* to promote workplace financial literacy at CFPB;

- Continued the "How Did I Get Here" series where Bureau leaders share stories and insights of how they made it to their current positions;

- Enhanced on-line learning and development resources, by adding access to thousands of on-line books and materials, as well as video vignettes of lessons learned from specialists, noted authors, and business leaders, as well as activating more online courses targeted to address the CFPB core competencies and basic supervisory skills, and added managerial learning references;

- Launched a library of online reference material through the CFPB library; and

- Refined a variety of examination tools, including: a full catalog of computer-based training modules on consumer compliance laws and regulations and general banking topics, a series of job aids that summarize important regulatory requirements, and access to a Regulatory Compliance Manual, which provides helpful commentary and explanation of consumer compliance regulatory requirements.

In addition, the Bureau is working to identify, cultivate, and sustain a diverse and inclusive work environment. The Bureau is committed to developing a culture that encourages collaboration and fairness, and leverages diversity throughout the organization so that all individuals are equipped to Serve, Lead, and Innovate.

# 10.3 Diversity and inclusion

In January 2012, the Bureau formally established the Office of Minority and Women Inclusion to ensure that diversity and inclusion continues to inform its work as provided under the Dodd-Frank Act.

OMWI focuses on developing and refining standards for:

- Equal employment opportunity, workforce diversity, and inclusion at all levels of the Bureau;

- Increased participation of minority-owned and women-owned businesses in the programs and contracts of the agency, including standards for coordinating technical assistance to such businesses; and

- Assessing the diversity policies and practices of entities regulated by the agency.

## 10.3.1 Diversity in the CFPB's workforce

As of September 30, 2014, the Bureau had 1,443 total employees. Women represent 47% of the Bureau's workforce. The CFPB is committed not only to strong workforce demographics by gender, but also to increasing the number of women in leadership positions. Along with gender equality, the Bureau aims to increase workforce diversity with greater representation of minorities. As Table 24 shows, minorities constituted 34% percent of the workforce at the end of Calendar Year 2013.

TABLE 24: CFPB WORKFORCE DIVERSITY FOR CALENDAR YEAR 2013

| Demographic group | CFPB CY2013 # | CFPB CY2013 # |
|---|---|---|
| Male | 698 | 53% |
| Female | 617 | 47% |
| | | |
| Non-Minority | 866 | 66% |
| Total Minority | 449 | 34% |
| Total Workforce | 1,315 | 100% |

Figure 13 shows the CFPB workforce by race and ethnicity. Of the 1,354 employees at year end of 2013, 69% self-identify as White, 16% as Black/African-American, 9% as Asian American, and just under 4% as another racial group or belonging to two or more racial groups. In terms of ethnicity, 5% of employees self-identify as Hispanic, and 95% as Non-Hispanic.

**FIGURE 13:** CFPB WORKFORCE BY ETHNICITY AND RACE FOR CALENDAR YEAR 2013

| Ethnic or racial group | CFPB CY2013 # | CFPB CY2013 # |
|---|---|---|
| Ethnic Group | | |
| Non-Hispanic | | 95% |
| Hispanic | | 5% |
| | | |
| Racial Group | | |
| White | | 69% |
| African American | 211 | 16% |
| Asian | 122 | 9% |
| American Indian or Alaska Native | 3 | 0.23% |
| Native Hawaiian or Pacific Islander | 2 | 0.15% |
| 2 or More Races | 38 | 3% |

## 10.3.2 OMWI's role at the CFPB

OMWI supports the Bureau's efforts to bring diverse perspectives to the CFPB's work by ensuring that the talents of employees are maximized and that inclusion strategies are incorporated into the policies, practices, and training at the Bureau. OMWI focuses on organizational culture by promoting collaboration and creativity and has embarked on several initiatives to better understand and improve the employee experience. OMWI is working to promote more inclusive hiring and contracting practices at the Bureau and comprehensive training that will enable managers and employees to both understand and appreciate diversity and how to foster an inclusive work environment.

## Inclusion

The CFPB is committed to fostering an environment in which every individual has an equitable opportunity to excel and contribute to the mission and goals of the Bureau. OMWI plans to optimize training and education to enhance diversity management and leadership skill sets. OMWI has established an executive diversity council consisting of Bureau-wide leaders to promote diversity and inclusion (D&I) practices throughout the Bureau. In conjunction with the council, a staff-level working group through which employees may communicate to management on broad-based diversity and inclusion insights and challenges, and participate in activities that increase awareness of D&I, is also currently being developed. The OMWI office has also launched a Bureau-wide newsletter to better connect with employees about the work of the office and to solicit strategies and recommendations from employees on ways to enhance the workforce cultural climate.

OMWI continues to provide diversity and inclusion training to Bureau employees to expand awareness, knowledge and cultural competencies to aid understanding of the value of a diverse workforce to the CFPB mission. As of the end of this reporting period, OMWI has provided diversity and inclusion training to most of the Bureau's workforce. The office will launch a mentoring program to equip employees with the tools necessary to navigate their career path. OMWI continues to collaborate with OHC and division heads to promote policies, practices, and procedures to ensure that all employees are developed to their maximum potential. OMWI works closely with OHC, the Office of Equal Employment Opportunity (OEEO), and department heads in analyzing annual employee survey results, exit survey trends, and workforce analytics to determine promotion and retention trends and areas of opportunity to maintain and grow an inclusive workforce at the CFPB.

## Workforce diversity

OMWI is responsible for promoting diverse and inclusive hiring practices at the Bureau. OMWI continues to collaborate with OHC and OEEO to develop tools to monitor and analyze the diversity of applicants and hires. OMWI participates in recruitment and outreach events in order to attract a diverse pool of qualified candidates emphasizing diversity from a wide range of American society. OMWI has developed strategic partnerships with colleges, universities, professional organizations and affinity groups that we believe will continue to connect us to a diverse applicant pool. OMWI has assisted with the development of internal systems and processes, as well as training, to ensure that the CFPB has the benefit of a diverse and qualified pool of candidates for all job openings. OMWI has formulated internal working groups that include members from each office to address specific areas for potential growth.

## Diversity and inclusion at regulated entities

Under the Dodd-Frank Act, OMWI is required to create standards for assessing the diversity and inclusion policies and practices of the entities regulated by the CFPB. OMWI continues to coordinate with fellow OMWI Directors at the FDIC, FRB, NCUA, OCC, and SEC to develop interagency standards. Draft standards were published in Fall 2013 and the agencies received public comment and feedback. OMWI Directors are currently working on finalized standards for release to the public.

## Procurement

OMWI and the Bureau's Procurement Office (Procurement) are committed to greater economic empowerment for women and minorities and aim to increase procurement opportunities for minority-owned and women-owned businesses.

OMWI has engaged in outreach efforts to raise awareness of procurement opportunities available at CFPB. These include:

- Creating and developing relationships with key business stakeholders, industry groups, and trade groups;

- Speaking at and attending supplier diversity events and co-locating with other Federal partners at events when available; and

- Developing literature and educational materials aimed at minority- and women-owned businesses.

The CFPB is a regular participant in an interagency working group consisting of other OMWI staff from the FDIC, FHFA, FRB, Treasury, NCUA, OCC, and SEC. In 2014, the CFPB and interagency partners participated in a series of procurement events targeted at recruiting diverse suppliers. The working group also developed joint materials including information on the OMWIs' directives to share with suppliers. Procurement is currently measuring obligations for certain small business contracts awarded to minority-owned small disadvantaged businesses and women-owned small businesses. As of the end of the fourth quarter in FY 2014,[116] the Bureau awarded 32% of contract dollars to small businesses.[117] As shown in Table 25, of the total contract dollars awarded in FY 2014, 10%[118] went to small disadvantaged businesses. Additionally, 11%[119] of total contract dollars went to woman-owned small businesses.

TABLE 25: CONTRACT DOLLARS AWARDED TO SMALL BUSINESS BY TYPE

|  | Obligated dollars* |
| --- | --- |
| Small business | $45,324,017 |
| Small disadvantaged business | $14,157,591 |
| Woman-owned small business | $15,327,669 |
| Service disabled veteran owned small business | $5,116,743 |
| HubZone small business | $2,889,320 |

*Dollars may apply to multiple socio-economic categories.

Coordinating with OMWI, Procurement has developed an external website presence with a forecast of procurement opportunities, in addition to a direct Procurement and OMWI email address that have fostered excellent communication between the office and potential small business vendors. Many small minority-owned and women-owned businesses may find trying to do business with the Federal government difficult and unclear. In an effort to increase transparency and enhance understanding, the CFPB has developed a number of practical resources for minority-owned businesses. OMWI has created brochures and pamphlets for diverse suppliers. These materials include information on historical obligations by products and

---

[116] Data source is from the Federal Procurement Data System (FPDS) for FY 2014 through September 30, 2014. The data was pulled, and is current, as of October 14, 2014. FPDS data is subject to an OMB annual validation each January for the previous fiscal year.

[117] Approximately $45 million.

[118] Approximately $14 million.

[119] Approximately $15 million.

service categories, a forecast of future procurements, and information on small business set-asides. The OMWI works with Procurement to make these resources available digitally and update them regularly on the CFPB's website.[120]

The two offices have also extended outreach efforts both locally and nationally, including presence at the National Minority Supplier Diversity Council, Annual Government Procurement Conference, National Minority Enterprise Development Week Conference, the Federal Reserve Board's Vendor Outreach Event, and the Womens' Business Enterprise National Council Annual Conference. In addition, OMWI and the Office of Procurement also holds a number of internal trainings targeted at minority owned and women owned businesses. For example, CFPB has held a small business outreach symposium, training sessions for non-profits navigating the Federal procurement process and a session on demystifying the government contracting process.

Finally, in furthering OMWI's mandate to ensure diversity and inclusion among its suppliers, OMWI and Procurement have developed a contractual provision concerning the "fair inclusion of women and minorities in the workforce of the contractor," and of subcontractors when applicable, as required under Section 342(c)(2) of the Dodd-Frank Act. In addition, Director Cordray has approved a CFPB Supplier Diversity Statement, reaffirming the Bureau's commitment to providing an environment of inclusion amongst qualified, diverse suppliers. The Statement can be seen in full on CFPB's external website.

## External Affairs/Consumer Education and Engagement

In collaboration with External Affairs and Consumer Education and Engagement, OMWI conducts outreach to consumer groups, advocacy organizations, and other stakeholders to develop strong and productive partnerships. The offices collaborate to reach consumers and potential candidates at recruiting events, community outreach events and others events. They also engage in meetings with these groups to discuss concerns and issues such as how policies may impact consumers, how they may improve contracting opportunities for minority and women-owned businesses and to learn about the consumer experience firsthand. OMWI will

---

[120] http://www.consumerfinance.gov/doing-business-with-us/ .

continue to develop productive relationships with the representatives of the communities that we serve.

## Diversity and inclusion challenges

The CFPB faces both the challenge and the opportunity of creating a federal agency from the ground up. This creation has come with its own series of growing pains and opportunities for improvement. In performing a standard internal management review, the CFPB detected significant difference between certain demographic groups in employee performance ratings for calendar year 2013.[121] After further analysis, the Bureau decided to move away from its existing performance management system, substitute an interim two-level system for two years, and work to develop a new performance management system going forward that would be consistent with the Bureau's commitment to excellence, equality and fairness. The Bureau also provided remediation to employees negatively affected by the former system. A review of Bureau systems has been procured from a third-party to provide additional analysis of fairness and equity concerns around a number of employee facing systems including performance management and compensation.

In addition to sharing results with the Collective Bargaining Representative, the NTEU, the Bureau has agreed to work together on developing a new performance rating system that will reflect our shared commitment to excellence. Further, to ensure the effectiveness of OMWI, Director Cordray has determined that the OMWI office should be housed in the Director's office and report directly to him, and take a leading role in ensuring that Diversity and Inclusion are prominent values within the Bureau.

In order to assess the current state of employee sentiment around issues of diversity, inclusion, equality and fairness, over the past quarter, Director Cordray directed OMWI to conduct listening sessions to hear employee feedback and to craft recommendations to him on the best ways to address those concerns. OMWI conducted 48 listening sessions and heard feedback from over 300 employees. OMWI transmitted its report and recommendations to the Director and the Bureau in August and the Director fully embraced the recommendations presented. The CFPB is fully committed to making sure that our talented and diverse staff is treated fairly and

---

[121] The Bureau conducts an annual employee survey and publicly posts the analysis of this survey on its website. The most recent report may be found in Appendix F.

with the respect they deserve. The Bureau will hold itself to the standards of fairness that we expect of the companies and industries we regulate.

The CFPB is also continuing to strengthen its efforts to hire a diverse workforce. Upon opening our doors in July 2011, the Bureau hired employees at a rapid pace in order to meet immediate requirements such as issuing regulations and building supervisory and enforcement capacity. While these efforts have yielded a comparatively diverse workforce, more can be done to maximize these efforts. The CFPB has made it a priority to cast a wide net to reach a large diverse applicant pool. The CFPB's outreach efforts and partnerships with minority-serving institutions and professional organizations serving minority populations reflect this commitment.

This continuous influx of new employees can make it challenging to identify an organizational culture. Additionally, challenges arise when balancing expectations of employees from the private sector with those from the public sector. A dispersed workforce throughout the United States further compounds challenges to create a cohesive work environment. Using data from the Annual Employee Survey and the Management Directive 715 on establishing and maintaining effective programs of equal employment opportunity, and other internal workforce reports (e.g. new hire, exit survey, etc.), the CFPB is developing strategies to support employee engagement and inclusion in the workplace as it matures out of the start-up phase. For example, OMWI has formed an executive-level diversity and inclusion council to help inform and foster the culture needed to support the CFPB's mission. OMWI is also developing an internal strategy to foster greater cohesion and further engage our regional staff with headquarters staff through an employee diversity council.

# APPENDIX A:

# More about the CFPB

**GENERAL INFORMATION:**

Email address: info@consumerfinance.gov

Phone number: (202) 435-7000

**WEBSITE:**

www.consumerfinance.gov

**MAILING ADDRESS:**

Consumer Financial Protection Bureau

ATTN: Employee name, Division, and/or Office Number

1700 G Street, NW

Washington, DC 20552

**CONSUMER COMPLAINTS AND QUESTIONS:**

Webpage: consumerfinance.gov/complaint

Toll free number: (855) 411-CFPB (2372)

TTY/TDD: (855) 729-CFPB (2372)

Fax number: (855) 237-2392

Hours of operation: 8 a.m. - 8 p.m. EST, services in 180+ languages

Consumer Financial Protection Bureau

PO Box 4503

Iowa City, Iowa 52244

**WHISTLEBLOWERS:**

Email: whistleblower@consumerfinance.gov

Toll free number: (855) 695-7974

**PRESS & MEDIA REQUESTS:**

Email: press@consumerfinance.gov

**OFFICE OF LEGISLATIVE AFFAIRS:**

Legislative Affairs: (202) 435-7960

**CFPB OMBUDSMAN'S OFFICE:**

Email: CFPBOmbudsman@cfpb.gov

Webpage: consumerfinance.gov/ombudsman

Toll free number: (855) 830-7880

TTY number: (202) 435-9835 Fax number: (202) 435-7888

# APPENDIX B:

# Statutory reporting requirements

This Appendix provides a guide to the Bureau's response to the reporting requirements of Section 1016(c) of the Dodd-Frank Act. The sections of the report identified below respond to Section 1016(c)'s requirements.

| Statutory Subsection | Reporting Requirement | Section | Page |
|---|---|---|---|
| 1 | A discussion of the significant problems faced by consumers in shopping for or obtaining consumer financial products or services | Consumer challenges in obtaining financial products and services – shopping challenges | 50-55 |
| 2 | A justification of the Bureau's budget request for the previous year | Budget; Appendix I – Financial and budget reports | 127-39 181-83 |
| 3 | A list of significant rules and orders adopted by the Bureau, as well as other significant initiatives conducted by the Bureau, during the preceding year, and the plan of the Bureau for rules, orders, or other initiatives to be undertaken during the upcoming period | Appendix C – Significant rules, orders, and initiatives | 157-66 |
| 4 | An analysis of complaints about consumer financial products or services that the Bureau has received and collected in its central database on complaints during the preceding year | Consumer challenges in obtaining financial products and services – Consumer concerns | 15-50 |

| | | | |
|---|---|---|---|
| 5 | A list, with a brief statement of the issues, of the public supervisory and enforcement actions to which the Bureau was a party during the preceding year | Enforcement actions | 100-13 |
| | | Fair lending enforcement actions | 117-21 |
| 6 | The actions taken regarding rules, orders, and supervisory actions with respect to covered persons which are not credit unions or depository institutions | Appendix D – Actions taken regarding rules, orders, and supervisory actions with respect to covered persons which are not credit unions or depository institutions | 167-69 |
| 7 | An assessment of significant actions by State attorneys general or State regulators relating to Federal consumer financial law | Appendix E – Significant state attorney general and regulator actions | 170-71 |
| 8 | An analysis of the Bureau's efforts to fulfill its fair lending mission | Fair lending | 114-23 |
| 9 | An analysis of the Bureau's efforts to increase workforce and contracting diversity consistent with the procedures established by OMWI | Diversity and excellence | 140-52 |

# APPENDIX C:

# Significant rules, orders, and initiatives[122]

Section 1016(c)(3) requires "a list of significant rules and orders adopted by the Bureau, as well as other significant initiatives conducted by the Bureau, during the preceding year and the plan of the Bureau for rules, orders or other initiatives to be undertaken during the upcoming period."

Below is a list of rules and other initiatives that the Bureau proposed, adopted or finalized during the preceding year.[123] Rather than limiting the list to significant items, the Bureau has, in order to be transparent and provide complete information about its activities, included a more expansive set of rules and initiatives:[124]

- Final rule: Defining Larger Participants of the International Money Transfer Market;[125]

- Proposed rule: Home Mortgage Disclosure (Regulation C); [126]

---

[122] Many links in this section are to documents published in the *Federal Register*. However, links to final rules, proposed rules and guidance documents may also be found on the CFPB's website, consumerfinance.gov/regulations/ and consumerfinance.gov/guidance.

[123] The preceding year is defined as October 1, 2013 - September 30, 2014.

[124] To better inform the public, this Appendix contains a discussion of a broad range of rulemakings, orders, and initiatives, which may not be defined as "significant" for other purposes. Items are listed in chronological order, beginning with the most recently-published document.

[125] http://www.gpo.gov/fdsys/pkg/FR-2014-09-23/pdf/2014-22310.pdf.

[126] This notice of proposed rulemaking, Docket CFPB-2014-0019, would amend 12 CFR Part 1003, and was published in the *Federal Register* on August 29, 2014. http://www.gpo.gov/fdsys/pkg/FR-2014-08-29/pdf/2014-18353.pdf.

- Final rule: Truth in Lending (Regulation Z) Annual Threshold Adjustments (CARD Act, HOEPA and ATR/QM);[127]

- Proposed policy statement: Disclosure of Consumer Complaint Data; [128]

- Final rule: Application of Regulation Z's Ability-to-Repay Rule to Certain Situations Involving Successors-in-Interest;[129]

- Final rule: Rules of Practice for Issuance of Temporary Cease-and-Desist Orders;[130]

- Request for Information Regarding the Use of Mobile Financial Services by Consumers and Its Potential for Improving the Financial Lives of Economically Vulnerable Consumers;[131]

- Proposed rule: Amendment to the Annual Privacy Notice Requirement Under the Gramm-Leach-Bliley Act (Regulation P);[132]

- Proposed rule: Amendments to the 2013 Mortgage Rules under the Truth in Lending Act (Regulation Z);[133]

---

[127] This final rule was published in the *Federal Register* on August 15, 2014. https://www.federalregister.gov/articles/2014/08/15/2014-18838/truth-in-lending-regulation-z-annual-threshold-adjustments-card-act-hoepa-and-atrqm.

[128] This notice and request for public comment was published in the *Federal Register* on July 23, 2014. https://www.federalregister.gov/articles/2014/08/04/2014-18355/disclosure-of-consumer-complaint-narrative-data.

[129] This final rule was published on the Bureau's website on July 8, 2014. http://files.consumerfinance.gov/f/201407_cfpb_bulletin_mortgage-lending-rules_successors.pdf.

[130] This final rule, Docket CFPB-2013-0030, amended 12 CFR Part 1081, and was published in the *Federal Register* on June 18, 2014. http://www.gpo.gov/fdsys/pkg/FR-2014-06-18/pdf/2014-14228.pdf.

[131] This request for information was published in the *Federal Register* on June 12, 2014. https://www.federalregister.gov/articles/2014/06/12/2014-13552/request-for-information-regarding-the-use-of-mobile-financial-services-by-consumers-and-its.

[132] This proposed rule was published in the *Federal Register* on May 13, 2014. http://www.gpo.gov/fdsys/pkg/FR-2014-05-13/pdf/2014-10713.pdf.

- Proposed rule: Electronic Fund Transfers (Regulation E);[134]

- Proposed rule: Minimum Requirements for Appraisal Management Companies;[135]

- Final Rule: Equal Access to Justice Act Implementation Rule; [136]

- Proposed rule: Defining Larger Participants of the International Money Transfer Market; [137]

- Request for Information Regarding the Mortgage Closing Process;[138]

- Final rule: Truth in Lending (Regulation Z): Adjustment To Asset-Size Exemption Threshold;[139]

- Final rule: Home Mortgage Disclosure (Regulation C): Adjustment To Asset-Size Exemption Threshold;[140]

---

[133] This prosed rule was published in the *Federal Register* on May 6, 2014.
https://www.federalregister.gov/articles/2014/05/06/2014-10207/amendments-to-the-2013-mortgage-rules-under-the-truth-in-lending-act-regulation-z.

[134] This proposed rule was published in the *Federal Register* on April 25, 2014.
https://www.federalregister.gov/articles/2014/04/25/2014-09036/electronic-fund-transfers-regulation-e.

[135] This joint notice of proposed rulemaking, Docket CFPB-2014-0006, would amend, among other parts, 12 CFR 1026, and was published in the *Federal Register* on April 9, 2014. http://www.gpo.gov/fdsys/pkg/FR-2014-04-09/pdf/2014-06860.pdf.

[136] This final rule, Docket CPFB-2012-0020, amended 12 CFR 1071 and was published in the *Federal Register* on February 10, 2014. http://www.gpo.gov/fdsys/pkg/FR-2014-02-10/pdf/2014-02115.pdf.

[137] This proposed rule, Docket CFPB-2014-0003, would amend 12 CFR 1090 and was published in the *Federal Register* on January 31, 2014. http://www.gpo.gov/fdsys/pkg/FR-2014-01-31/pdf/2014-01606.pdf.

[138] This notice was published in the *Federal Register* on January 1, 2014.
https://www.federalregister.gov/articles/2014/01/03/2013-31436/request-for-information-regarding-the-mortgage-closing-process.

[139] This final rule amended 12 CFR 1026 and was published in the *Federal Register* on December 30, 2013. http://www.gpo.gov/fdsys/pkg/FR-2013-12-30/pdf/2013-31225.pdf.

[140] This final rule amended 12 CFR Part 1003 and was published in the *Federal Register* on December 30, 2013. http://www.gpo.gov/fdsys/pkg/FR-2013-12-30/pdf/2013-31223.pdf.

- Final rule: Appraisals for Higher-Priced Mortgage Loans;[141]

- Final rule: Integrated Mortgage Disclosures under the Real Estate Settlement Procedures Act (Regulation X) and the Truth In Lending Act (Regulation Z);[142]

- Final rule: Truth in Lending (Regulation Z);[143]

- Final rule: Defining Larger Participants of the Student Loan Servicing Market;[144]

- Final rule: Consumer Leasing (Regulation M);[145]

- Finale rule: Truth in Lending (Regulation Z);[146]

- Advance notice of proposed rulemaking: Debt Collection (Regulation F);[147]

- Final Policy to Encourage Trial Disclosure Programs; Information Collection;[148]

- Proposed Interagency Policy Statement Establishing Joint Standards for Assessing the Diversity Policies and Practices of Entities Regulated by the Agencies;[149]

---

[141] This supplemental final rule, Docket CFPB-2013-0020, amended 12 CFR Part 1026 and was published in the *Federal Register* on December 26, 2013. http://www.gpo.gov/fdsys/pkg/FR-2013-12-26/pdf/2013-30108.pdf.

[142] This final rule, Docket CFPB-2012-0028, amended 12 CFR Parts 1024 and 1026 and was published in the *Federal Register* on December 31, 2013. http://www.gpo.gov/fdsys/pkg/FR-2013-12-31/pdf/2013-28210.pdf.

[143] This final rule amended 12 CFR Part 1026 and was published in the *Federal Register* on December 16, 2013. http://www.gpo.gov/fdsys/pkg/FR-2013-12-16/pdf/2013-29844.pdf.

[144] This final rule, Docket CFPB-2013-0005, amended 12 CFR 1090 and was published in the *Federal Register* on December 6, 2013. http://www.gpo.gov/fdsys/pkg/FR-2013-12-06/pdf/2013-29145.pdf.

[145] This joint final rule amended 12 CFR 213 and 12 CFR 1013 and was published in the *Federal Register* on November 25, 2013. http://www.gpo.gov/fdsys/pkg/FR-2013-11-25/pdf/2013-28194.pdf.

[146] This joint final rule amended 12 CFR Parts 226 and 1026 and was published in the *Federal Register* on November 25, 2013. http://www.gpo.gov/fdsys/pkg/FR-2013-11-25/pdf/2013-28195.pdf.

[147] This advance notice of proposed rulemaking with request for public comment, Docket CFPB-2013-0033, would amend 12 CFR Part 1006 and was published in the *Federal Register* on November 12, 2013. http://www.gpo.gov/fdsys/pkg/FR-2013-11-12/pdf/2013-26875.pdf.

[148] This Notice of policy, Docket CFPB-2012-0046, was published in the *Federal Register* on October 29, 2013. http://www.gpo.gov/fdsys/pkg/FR-2013-10-29/pdf/2013-25580.pdf.

- Interim final rule with request for public comment: Amendments to the 2013 Mortgage Rules under the Real Estate Settlement Procedures Act (Regulation X) and the Truth in Lending Act (Regulation Z);[150] and

- Final rule: Amendments to the 2013 Mortgage Rules under the Equal Credit Opportunity Act (Regulation B), Real Estate Settlement Procedures Act (Regulation X), and the Truth in Lending Act (Regulation Z).[151]

In the upcoming period, the Bureau also intends to propose or adopt the following rules and orders, and conduct the following initiatives:

- Rules finalizing the restatement of regulations implementing consumer financial protection laws transferred from other regulatory agencies to the Bureau by the Dodd-Frank Act;

- Continue work on a proposal to seek comment on whether to extend the sunset on a Dodd-Frank Act provision that allows depository institutions to estimate certain remittances disclosure information under certain circumstances;

- Continue work to address issues in connection with implementation of the Dodd-Frank Act's mortgage requirements and implementation of the Bureau's January 2013 mortgage rules;

- Continue work toward a final rulemaking to implement the Dodd-Frank Act amendments to HMDA;

- Continue work toward a rulemaking on general purpose reloadable prepaid cards;

---

[149] This Notice of Proposed Interagency Policy Statement with Request for Comment, Docket CFPB-2013-0029, was published in the *Federal Register* on October 25, 2013. http://www.gpo.gov/fdsys/pkg/FR-2013-10-25/pdf/2013-25142.pdf.

[150] This interim final rule, Docket CFPB-2013-0031, amended 12 CFR Parts 1024 and 1026 and was published in the *Federal Register* on October 23, 2013. http://www.gpo.gov/fdsys/pkg/FR-2013-10-23/pdf/2013-24521.pdf.

[151] This final rule, Docket CFPB-2013-0018, amended 12 CFR Parts 1002, 1024, and 1026 and was published in the *Federal Register* on October 1, 2013. http://www.gpo.gov/fdsys/pkg/FR-2013-10-01/pdf/2013-22752.pdf.

- Continued expansion of the Bureau's capacity to handle consumer complaints with respect to all products and services within its authority;

- Enforcement of Nondiscrimination on the Basis of Disability in Programs Receiving Financial Assistance from the Bureau;

- Propose additional rules to further define the scope of the Bureau's nonbank supervision program; and

- Working jointly with the FRB, rules finalizing a Board proposal regarding the Expedited Funds Availability Act as implemented by Regulation CC.

The Bureau has issued the following bulletins and guidance documents over the past year:[152]

- Interagency Guidance Regarding Unfair or Deceptive Credit Practices;[153]

- Bulletin 2014-01 on Mortgage Servicing Transfers;[154]

- Policy Guidance on Supervisory and Enforcement Considerations Relevant to Mortgage Brokers Transitioning to Mini-Correspondent Lenders;[155]

- Application of Regulation Z's Ability-to-Repay Rule to Certain Situations Involving Successors-in-Interest;[156]

- Bulletin 2014-01 on the FCRA's requirement that furnishers conduct investigations of disputed information;[157]

---

[152] The past year is defined here as October 1, 2013 – September 30, 2014. The Bureau posts all bulletins and guidance documents on its website, consumerfinance.gov.

[153] This document was issued jointly by the FRB, CFPB, FDIC, NCUA, and OCC on August 22, 2014. http://www.gpo.gov/fdsys/pkg/FR-2014-08-29/pdf/2014-18353.pdf.

[154] CFPB Bulletin 2014-01 was published to the Bureau's website on August 19, 2014. http://files.consumerfinance.gov/f/201408_cfpb_bulletin_mortgage-servicing-transfer.pdf.

[155] This document was published on the Bureau's website on July 11, 2014. http://files.consumerfinance.gov/f/201407_cfpb_guidance_mini-correspondent-lenders.pdf.

[156] This final rule was published on the Bureau's website on July 8, 2014. http://files.consumerfinance.gov/f/201407_cfpb_bulletin_mortgage-lending-rules_successors.pdf.

- Final rule defining "larger participants" of the student loan servicing market;[158]

- FFIEC Guidance on Social Media;[159]

- Bulletin 2013-13 to provide guidance to lenders regarding the homeownership counseling list requirement finalized in High-Cost Mortgage and Homeownership Counseling Amendments to the TILA (Regulation Z) and Homeownership Counseling Amendments to the RESPA Housing Counselor Amendments Final Rule;[160]

- Interagency Statement on Fair Lending Compliance and the Ability-to-Repay and Qualified Mortgage Standards Rule;[161]

- Bulletin 2013-12 to provide implementation guidance in implementing certain of the 2013 RESPA and TILA Servicing Final Rules;[162]

- Bulletin 2013-11 on HMDA and Regulation C – Compliance Management; CFPB HMDA Resubmission Schedule and Guidelines; and HMDA Enforcement;[163] and

- HMDA Resubmission Schedule and Guidelines to be used to verify the accuracy of institution-reported HMDA data during HMDA reviews and to describe when institutions should be required to correct and resubmit HMDA data.[164]

---

[157] CFPB Bulletin 2014-01 was published to the Bureau's website on February 27, 2014.
http://files.consumerfinance.gov/f/201402_cfpb_bulletin_fair-credit-reporting-act.pdf.

[158] http://www.gpo.gov/fdsys/pkg/FR-2013-12-06/pdf/2013-29145.pdf.

[159] http://files.consumerfinance.gov/f/201309_cfpb_social_media_guidance.pdf.

[160] CFPB Bulletin 2013-13 was published to the Bureau's website on November 8, 2013.
http://files.consumerfinance.gov/f/201311_cfpb_bulletin_homeownership-counseling-list-requirements.pdf.

[161] This document was released on October 22, 2013.
http://files.consumerfinance.gov/f/201310_cfpb_guidance_qualified-mortgage-fair-lending-risks.pdf.

[162] CFPB Bulletin 2013-12 was published to the Bureau's website on October 15, 2013.
http://files.consumerfinance.gov/f/201310_cfpb_mortgage-servicing_bulletin.pdf.

[163] CFPB Bulletin 2013-11 was published to the Bureau's website on October 9, 2013.
http://files.consumerfinance.gov/f/201310_cfpb_hmda_compliance-bulletin_fair-lending.pdf.

The Bureau has issued the following orders to remedy violations of Federal consumer financial protection law over the past year:[165]

- *In the Matter of: Lighthouse Title, Inc.;*[166]

- *In the Matter of: Flagstar Bank, F.S.B.;*[167]

- *In the Matter of: U.S. Bank N.A.;*[168]

- *In the Matter of: First Investors Financial Services Group, Inc.;*[169]

- *In the Matter of: USA Discounters, Ltd.;*[170]

- *In the Matter of: Amerisave Mortgage Corporation, et al.;*[171]

- *In the Matter of: Colfax Capital Corp., et al.;*[172]

- *In the Matter of: ACE Cash Express, Inc.;*[173]

---

[164] This document was published on the Bureau's website on October 9, 2013.
http://files.consumerfinance.gov/f/201310_cfpb_hmda_resubmission-guidelines_fair-lending.pdf.

[165] October 1, 2013 – September 30, 2014.

[166] File No. 2014-CFPB-0015. Consent order entered September 30, 2014.
http://files.consumerfinance.gov/f/201409_cfpb_consent-order_lighthouse-title.pdf.

[167] File No. 2014-CFPB-0014. Consent order entered September 29, 2014.
http://files.consumerfinance.gov/f/201409_cfpb_consent-order_flagstar.pdf.

[168] File No. 2014-CFPB-0013. Consent order entered September 25, 2014.
http://files.consumerfinance.gov/f/201409_cfpb_consent-order_us-bank.pdf.

[169] File No. 2014-CFPB-0012. Consent order entered August 20, 2014.
http://files.consumerfinance.gov/f/201408_cfpb_consent-order_first-investors.pdf.

[170] File No. 2014-CFPB-0011. Consent order entered August 14, 2014.
http://files.consumerfinance.gov/f/201408_cfpb_consent-order_usa-discounters.pdf.

[171] File No. 2014-CFPB-0010. Consent order entered August 12, 2014.
http://files.consumerfinance.gov/f/201408_cfpb_consent-order_amerisave.pdf.

[172] File No. 2014-CFPB-0009. Consent order entered July 29, 2014.
http://files.consumerfinance.gov/f/201407_cfpb_consent-order_rome-finance.pdf.

- *In the Matter of: Synchrony Bank, f/k/a GE Capital Retail Bank;*[174]

- *In the Matter of: Stonebridge Title Services, Inc.;*[175]

- *In the Matter of: JRHBW Realty, Inc., d/b/a RealtySouth; TitleSouth, LLC;*[176]

- *In the Matter of: Bank of America, N.A., and FIA Card Services, N.A.;*[177]

- *In the Matter of: 1st Alliance Lending, LLC;*[178]

- *In the Matter of: Fidelity Mortgage Corporation and Mark Figert;*[179]

- *In the Matters of: American Express Centurion Bank, et al.;*[180]

- *In the Matter of: Ally Financial Inc.; and Ally Bank;*[181]

---

[173] File No. 2014-CFPB-0008. Consent order filed on July 10, 2014.
http://files.consumerfinance.gov/f/201407_cfpb_consent-order_ace-cash-express.pdf.

[174] File No. 2014-CFPB-0007. Consent order filed on June 19, 2014.
http://files.consumerfinance.gov/f/201406_cfpb_consent-order_synchrony-bank.pdf.

[175] File No. 2014-CFPB-0006. Consent order filed on June 12, 2014.
http://files.consumerfinance.gov/f/201406_cfpb_consent-order_stonebridge-title-services.pdf.

[176] File No. 2014-CFPB-0005. Consent order filed May 28, 2014.
http://files.consumerfinance.gov/f/201405_cfpb_consent-order_realty-south-and-title-south.pdf.

[177] File No. 2014-CFPB-004. Consent order filed April 9, 2014.
http://files.consumerfinance.gov/f/201404_cfpb_bankofamerica_consent-order.pdf.

[178] File No. 2014-CFPB-0003. Consent order filed on February 24, 2014.
http://files.consumerfinance.gov/f/201402_cfpb_consent-order_first-alliance.pdf.

[179] 2014-CFPB-0001. Consent order filed on January 16, 2014.
http://files.consumerfinance.gov/f/201401_cfpb_consent-order_fidelity.pdf.

[180] Files 2013-CFPB-0011, http://files.consumerfinance.gov/f/201312_cfpb_consent_amex_centurion_011.pdf,
2013-CFPB-0012, http://files.consumerfinance.gov/f/201312_cfpb_consent_amex_FSB_012.pdf, and 2013-CFPB-
0013, http://files.consumerfinance.gov/f/201312_CFPB_Consent_AETRS_013.pdf were entered on December 24,
2013.

[181] File 2013-CFPB-0010. Consent order filed on December 20, 2013.
http://files.consumerfinance.gov/f/201312_cfpb_consent-order_ally.pdf.

- *In the Matter of: GE Capital Retail Bank, CareCredit LLC;*[182]

- *In the Matter of: 3D Resorts-Bluegrass, LLC;*[183]

- *In the Matter of: Cash America International, Inc.;*[184]

- *In the Matter of: Washington Federal;*[185] and

- *In the Matter of: Mortgage Master.*[186]

---

[182] File 2013-CFPB-0009. Consent order filed on December 10, 2013.
http://files.consumerfinance.gov/f/201312_cfpb_consent-order_ge-carecredit.pdf.

[183] File 2013-CFPB-0002. Consent order filed on December 3, 2013.
http://files.consumerfinance.gov/f/201312_cfpb_consent-order_3dresorts-bluegrass.pdf.

[184] File 2013-CFPB-0008. Consent order filed on November 20, 2013.
http://files.consumerfinance.gov/f/201311_cfpb_cashamerica_consent-order.pdf.

[185] File 2013-CFPB-0005. Consent order filed on October 9, 2013.
http://files.consumerfinance.gov/f/201310_cfpb_consent-order_washington-federal.pdf.

[186] File 2013-CFPB-0006. Consent order filed on October 9, 2013.
http://files.consumerfinance.gov/f/201310_cfpb_consent-order_mortgage-master.pdf.

# APPENDIX D:

# Actions taken regarding rules, orders, and supervisory actions with respect to covered persons which are not credit unions or depository institutions

Section 1016(c)(6) requires a report on "the actions taken regarding rules, orders and supervisory actions with respect to covered persons which are not credit unions or depository institutions." Between October 1, 2013 and September 30, 2014, the Bureau has taken the following actions with respect to such covered persons:

- *In the Matter of: Mortgage Master, Inc.* (File No. 2013-CFPB-0006) (consent order entered October 9, 2013);

- *In the Matter of: Cash America International, Inc.* (File No. 2013-CFPB-0008) (consent order entered November 20, 2013);

- *In the Matter of: 3D Resorts-Bluegrass, LLC*, File No. 2013-CFPB-0002 (consent order entered December 2, 2013);

- *In the Matter of CareCredit LLC* (File No. 2013-CFPB-0009) (consent order entered December 10, 2013);

- *In the Matter of: Fidelity Mortgage Corporation and Mark Figert* (File No. 2014-CFPB-0001) (consent order entered January 16, 2014);

- *In the Matter of: 1st Alliance Lending, LLC* (File No. 2014-CFPB-0003) (consent order filed on February 24, 2014);

- *In the Matter of: JRHBW Realty, Inc., doing business as RealtySouth; TitleSouth, LLC* (File No. 2014-CFPB-0005) (consent order filed May 28, 2014);

- *In the Matter of:* Stonebridge Title Services, Inc. (File No. 2014-CFPB-0006) (consent order filed on June 12, 2014);[187]

- *In the Matter of: ACE Cash Express, Inc.* (File No. 2014-CFPB-0008) (consent order filed on July 8, 2014);[188]

- *In the Matter of: Colfax Capital Corp., et al.* (File No. 2012-CFPB-0009) (consent order entered July 29, 2014);[189]

- *In the Matter of: Amerisave Mortgage Corporation, et al.* (File No. 2014-CFPB-0010) (consent order entered August 12, 2014);[190]

- *In the Matter of: USA Discounters, Ltd.* (File No. 2014-CFPB-0011) (consent order entered August 13, 2014);[191]

- *In the Matter of: First Investors Financial Services Group, Inc.* (File No. 2014-CFPB-0012) (consent order entered August 20, 2014);[192]

- *In the Matter of: Lighthouse Title, Inc.* (File No. 2014-CFPB-0015) (consent order entered September 30, 2014);[193] and

- The Bureau's *Supervisory Highlights* publications provide general information about the Bureau's supervisory activities at banks and nonbanks without identifying specific

---

[187] http://files.consumerfinance.gov/f/201406_cfpb_consent-order_stonebridge-title-services.pdf.

[188] http://files.consumerfinance.gov/f/201407_cfpb_consent-order_ace-cash-express.pdf.

[189] http://files.consumerfinance.gov/f/201407_cfpb_consent-order_rome-finance.pdf.

[190] http://files.consumerfinance.gov/f/201408_cfpb_consent-order_amerisave.pdf.

[191] http://files.consumerfinance.gov/f/201408_cfpb_consent-order_usa-discounters.pdf.

[192] http://files.consumerfinance.gov/f/201408_cfpb_consent-order_first-investors.pdf.

[193] http://files.consumerfinance.gov/f/201409_cfpb_consent-order_lighthouse-title.pdf.

companies. The Bureau published three issues of *Supervisory Highlights* between October 1, 2013 and September 30, 2014.[194]

---

[194] **Winter 2013:** http://www.consumerfinance.gov/reports/supervisory-highlights-winter-2013/; **Spring 2014:** http://www.consumerfinance.gov/reports/supervisory-highlights-spring-2014/; **and Summer 2014:** http://www.consumerfinance.gov/reports/supervisory-highlights-summer-2014/.

# APPENDIX E:

# Significant state attorney general and regulator actions

Dodd-Frank Section 1016(c)(7) requires "an assessment of significant actions by State attorneys general or State regulators relating to Federal consumer financial law." The reporting period for this information is October 1, 2013 – September 30, 2014.

For purposes of the Section 1016(c)(7) reporting requirement at this early period in the Bureau's development, the Bureau has determined that any actions asserting claims pursuant to Section 1042 of the Dodd-Frank Act are "significant." The Bureau is aware of the following State Attorney General actions that were initiated during the reporting period and that asserted Dodd-Frank Act claims:

- *People of the State of Illinois, by Lisa Madigan, Illinois Attorney General, v. CMK Investments, INC d/b/a All Credit Lenders, Inc., an Illinois Corporation*, No. 2014CH04694 (Cir. Ct. Cook Cnty. Mar. 18, 2014), *removed* No. 14-cv-02783 (N.D. Ill. Apr. 17, 2014).
- *People of the State of Illinois, by Lisa Madigan, Illinois Attorney General, v. Alta Colleges, Inc., a Delaware Corporation, Westwood College, Inc., a Colorado Corporation d/b/a Westwood College and Westwood College Online; Wesgray Corporation, a Colorado corporation d/b/a/ Westwood College-River Oaks and Westwood College-Chicago Loop; Elbert, Inc., a Colorado Corporation d/b/a Westwood College-DuPage; and El Nell Inc., a Colorado corporation d/b/a Westwood College-O'Hare Airport*, No. 2012CH01587 (Cir. Ct. Cook Cnty. Mar. 20, 2014), *removed* No.1-cv-3786 (N.D. Ill. May 22, 2014).
- *Benjamin M. Lawskey, Superintendent of Financial Services of the State of New York, v. Condor Capital Corporation and Stephen Baron*, No. 14 CV 2863 (S.D.N.Y. Apr. 25, 2014).

- *State of Mississippi ex rel. Jim Hood, Attorney General of the State of Mississippi v. Experian Information Solutions, Inc.*, No. 14-1212(4) (Ch. Ct. Harrison Cty. May 16, 2014), *removed* No. 14-cv-00243-LG-JMR (S.D. Miss. June 12, 2014).

# APPENDIX F:

# Reports

The CFPB published the following reports from October 1, 2013 through September 30, 2014, which may be found at consumerfinance.gov/reports/:

**October 1, 2013**: CARD Act report: A review of the impact of the CARD Act on the consumer credit card market;

**October 16, 2013**: Annual report of the CFPB student loan ombudsman;

**November 5, 2013**: Semi-Annual Report of the Consumer Financial Protection Bureau;

**November 5, 2013**: Consumer Financial Protection Bureau Independent Audit of Selected Operations and Budget;

**November 14, 2013**: Empowering low income and economically vulnerable consumers: report on a national convening;

**November 18, 2013**: Navigating the market: A comparison of spending on financial education and financial marketing;

**November 22, 2013**: Understanding the effects of certain deposit regulations on financial institutions' operations: Findings on relative costs for systems, personnel, and processes at seven institutions;

**December 12, 2013**: Arbitration study preliminary results: Section 1028(a) study results to date;

**December 13, 2013**: 2013 CFPB annual employee survey;

**December 16, 2013**: Financial report of the Consumer Financial Protection Bureau;

**December 17, 2013**: College credit card agreements: Annual report to Congress;

**December 30, 2013**: Report of the Consumer Financial Protection Bureau pursuant to section 1017(e)(4) of the Dodd-Frank Act;

**January 13, 2014**: Growing our human capital: Human Capital Annual report to Congress;

**January 24, 2014**: Rigorous evaluation of financial capability strategies: Why, when and how. Perspectives from the field;

**January 30, 2014**: Supervisory Highlights: Winter 2013;

**February 27, 2014**: Credit reporting complaint snapshot;

**March 5, 2014**: Complaints received from servicemembers, veterans, and their families. A snapshot by the Office of Servicemember Affairs;

**March 12, 2014**: Annual FOIA report of the Consumer Financial Protection Bureau;

**March 12, 2014**: Chief FOIA Officer report of the Consumer Financial Protection Bureau;

**March 20, 2014**: Fair Debt Collection Practices Act: CFPB annual report 2014;

**March 25, 2014**: CFPB data point: Payday lending;

**March 28, 2014**: No FEAR Act annual report FY 2013. Pursuant to Notification and Federal Employee Antidiscrimination and Retaliation Act of 2002;

**March 31, 2014**: Consumer Response annual report: January 1 – December 31, 2013;

**April 4, 2014**: Office of Minority and Women Inclusion annual report;

**April 22, 2014**: Mid-year update on student loan complaints;

**April 22, 2014**: Mortgage closings today: A preliminary look at the role of technology in improving the closing process for consumers;

**April 30, 2014**: Fair Lending report of the Consumer Financial Protection Bureau;

**May 7, 2014**: Snapshot of older consumers and mortgage debt;

**May 20, 2014**: Data point: Medical debt and credit scores;

**May 22, 2014**: Supervisory Highlights: Spring 2014;

**May 28, 2014**: Semi-Annual Report of the Consumer Financial Protection Bureau;

**July 3, 2014**: Report on the use of remittance histories in credit scoring;

**July 16, 2014**: Consumer Response: A snapshot of complaints received;

**July 17, 2014**: 2014 Financial literacy annual report;

**July 29, 2014**: Plain Writing Act compliance report 2014;

**July 31, 2014**: Data point: Checking account overdraft;

**August 21, 2014**: Building financial capability in youth employment programs;

**August 26, 2014**: Financial wellness at work: a review of promising practices and policies;

**September 17, 2014**: Supervisory Highlights: Summer 2014;

**September 17, 2014**: Using publicly available information to proxy for unidentified race and ethnicity; **and**

**September 30, 2014**: Manufactured-housing consumer finance in the United States.

# APPENDIX G:

# Congressional testimony

Senior CFPB staff has testified before Congress a total of 52 times since it began in 2011, including on the following nine occasions between October 1, 2013 and September 30, 2014, which may be found at http://www.consumerfinance.gov/newsroom/?type=testimony:

**November 12, 2013**: Richard Cordray before the Senate Committee on Banking, Housing, and Urban Affairs. "The Consumer Financial Protection Bureau's Semi-Annual Report to Congress";

**November 20, 2013**: Hollister K. Petraeus before the Senate Committee on Commerce, Science, & Transportation. "Soldiers as Consumers: Predatory and Unfair Business Practices Harming the Military Community";

**January 28, 2014**: Richard Cordray before the House Committee on Financial Services. "The Semi-Annual Report of the Consumer Financial Protection Bureau";

**April 8, 2014**: Meredith Fuchs before the House Committee on Financial Services. "Who's in Your Wallet: Examining How Washington Red Tape Impairs Economic Freedom";

**June 4, 2014**: Rohit Chopra before the Senate Committee on the Budget. "The Impact of Student Loan Debt on Borrowers and the Economy";

**June 9, 2014**: Richard Cordray before the Senate Committee on Banking, Housing and Urban Affairs. "The Consumer Financial Protection Bureau's Semi-Annual Report to Congress";

**June 18, 2014**: Richard Cordray before the House Committee on Financial Services. "The Semi-Annual Report of the Consumer Financial Protection Bureau";

**July 30, 2014**: Richard Cordray before the House Committee on Financial Services Subcommittee on Oversight and Investigations. "Allegations of Discrimination and Retaliation and the CFPB Management Culture"; **and**

**September 9, 2014**: Richard Cordray before the Senate Committee on Banking, Housing and Urban Affairs. "Wall Street Reform: Assessing and Enhancing the Financial Regulatory System".

# APPENDIX H:

# Speeches

Director Richard Cordray or Deputy Director Steve Antonakes spoke at the following public events between October 1, 2013 and September 30, 2014:[195]

**October 2, 2013**: Remarks by Richard Cordray at the CARD Act Field Hearing in Chicago, IL;

**October 3, 2013**: Remarks by Richard Cordray at the Annual Financial Literacy and Economic Education Conference in Baltimore, MD;

**October 9, 2013**: Remarks by Steve Antonakes at the FDIC Advisory Committee on Economic Inclusion in Washington, DC;

**October 21, 2013**: Remarks by Richard Cordray at the American Bankers Association Annual Convention in New Orleans, LA;

**October 23, 2013**: Remarks by Richard Cordray at the Financial Literacy and Education Commission Meeting in Washington, DC;

**October 28, 2013**: Remarks by Richard Cordray at the Mortgage Bankers Association Annual Convention in Washington, DC;

**November 14, 2013**: Remarks by Richard Cordray at the CFPB Auto Finance Forum in Washington, DC;

**November 20, 2013**: Remarks by Richard Cordray at the "Know Before You Owe" Mortgage Field Hearing in Boston, MA;

---

[195] All speeches by CFPB senior staff are available at: http://www.consumerfinance.gov/newsroom/?type=speech-2.

**November 21, 2013**: Remarks by Richard Cordray at The Clearing House Annual Conference in New York, NY;

**December 5, 2013**: Remarks by Richard Cordray at the Consumer Federation of America;

**December 12, 2013**: Remarks by Richard Cordray at the Field Hearing on Arbitration in Dallas, TX;

**January 7, 2014**: Remarks by Richard Cordray at the National Association of Realtors in Washington, DC;

**January 10, 2014**: Remarks by Richard Cordray at the Fielding Hearing on Mortgages in Phoenix, AZ;

**January 22, 2014**: Remarks by Richard Cordray at the U.S. Conference of Mayors in Washington, DC;

**February 12, 2014**: Remarks by Richard Cordray at the Financial Literacy and Education Commission in Washington, DC;

**February 19, 2014**: Remarks by Steve Antonakes at the Mortgage Bankers Association in Orlando, FL;

**February 25, 2014**: Remarks by Richard Cordray at the Financial Literacy and Education Commission Field Hearing in Atlanta, GA;

**February 26, 2014**: Remarks by Richard Cordray at the National Association of Attorneys General Winter Meeting in Washington, DC;

**February 27, 2014**: Remarks by Richard Cordray at the Consumer Advisory Board Meeting in Washington, DC;

**March 3, 2014**: Remarks by Steve Antonakes at Protecting Nevada's Consumers: A Common Ground Conference in Las Vegas, NV;

**March 10, 2014**: Remarks by Richard Cordray at the President's Advisory Council Meeting in Washington, DC;

**March 12, 2014**: Remarks by Steve Antonakes at the National Community Reinvestment Coalition Annual Conference in Washington, DC;

**March 18, 2014**: Remarks by Richard Cordray at the National Association of State Treasurers Legislative Conference in Washington, DC;

**March 19, 2014**: Remarks by Steve Antonakes at the U.S. Chamber of Commerce in Washington, DC;

**March 25, 2014**: Remarks by Richard Cordray at the Payday Field Hearing in Nashville, TN;

**April 3, 2014**: Remarks by Richard Cordray at the American Bar Association in Washington, DC;

**April 4, 2014:** Remarks by Richard Cordray at the Greenlining Institute's Economic Summit in Oakland, CA;

**April 7, 2014:** Remarks by Richard Cordray at the Federal Reserve Bank of Chicago in Chicago, IL;

**April 8, 2014:** Remarks by Richard Cordray at the Jump$tart Coalition Awards Dinner in Washington, DC;

**April 23, 2014**: Remarks by Richard Cordray at the Mortgage Closing Forum in Washington, DC;

**May 9, 2014**: Remarks by Richard Cordray at the Federal Reserve Bank of Chicago in Chicago, IL;

**May 19, 2014**: Remarks by Richard Cordray at the 2014 Boulder Summer Conference on Financial Decision Making in Boulder, CO;

**May 29, 2014**: Remarks by Richard Cordray at the Financial Literacy and Education Commission Meeting in Washington, DC;

**June 9, 2014**: Remarks by Steve Antonakes at the American Bankers Association Regulatory Compliance Conference in New Orleans, LA;

**June 11, 2014**: Remarks by Richard Cordray at the Mobile Request for Information Field Hearing in New Orleans, LA;

**June 16, 2014**: Remarks by Richard Cordray at the Marian J. Mohr Memorial Library in Johnston, RI;

**June 18, 2014**: Remarks by Steve Antonakes at the Consumer Advisory Board Meeting in Reno, NV;

**July 9, 2014**: Remarks by Richard Cordray at the U.S. Programme for International Student Assessment Financial Literacy Data Release in Washington, DC;

**July 16, 2014**: Remarks by Richard Cordray at the Consumer Response Field Hearing in El Paso, TX;

**August 18, 2014**: Remarks by Richard Cordray at the Association of Military Banks of America Fall Workshop in Washington, DC;

**September 18, 2014:** Remarks by Richard Cordray at the Auto Finance Field Hearing in Indianapolis, IN; **and**

**September 29, 2014:** Remarks by Richard Cordray at the Society for Financial Education and Professional Development in Arlington, VA.

# APPENDIX I:

# Financial and budget reports

The CFPB has published the following financial reports from January 1, 2012 through September 30, 2014, which are all available at consumerfinance.gov/budget:

**January 20, 2012**: CFO update for the first quarter of FY 2012;

**May 11, 2012**: CFO update for the second quarter of FY 2012;

**July 27, 2012**: CFO update for the third quarter of FY 2012;

**November 15, 2012**: Financial Report of the CFPB – FY 2012;

**December 15, 2012**: CFO Update for the fourth quarter of FY 2012;

**February 15, 2013**: CFO Update for the first quarter of FY 2013;

**May 15, 2013**: CFO Update for the second quarter of FY 2013;

**August 15, 2013**: CFO Update for the third quarter of FY 2013;

**December 15, 2013**: Financial Report of the CFPB – FY 2013;

**December 15, 2013**: CFO Update for the fourth quarter of FY 2013;

**February 14, 2014**: CFO Update for the first quarter of FY 2014;

**May 15, 2014**: CFO Update for the second quarter of FY 2014;

**August 15, 2014**: CFO Update for the third quarter of FY 2014;

**November 15, 2014:** Financial Report of the CFPB – FY 2014;[196] **and**

**November 15, 2014:** CFO Update for the fourth quarter of FY 2014.[197]

The CFPB has published the following Budget Documents, which are all available at consumerfinance.gov/budget:

- Fiscal Year 2012 Budget in Brief;

- Fiscal Year 2012 Congressional Budget Justification;

- Fiscal Year 2013 Budget in Brief;

- FY 2013 Budget Justification;

- FY 2014 CFPB Strategic Plan, Budget, and Performance Report; **and**

- FY 2015 CFPB Strategic Plan, Budget, and Performance Report.

The CFPB has published the following funding requests to and funding acknowledgements from the Federal Reserve Board, from January 1, 2012 through July 28, 2014, which are all available at consumerfinance.gov/budget:

**January 6, 2012:** Funding Acknowledgement from the Federal Reserve Board;

**March 30, 2012:** Funding Request to the Federal Reserve Board;

**April 5, 2012:** Funding Acknowledgement from the Federal Reserve Board;

**July 2, 2012:** Funding Request to the Federal Reserve Board;

**July 9, 2012:** Funding Acknowledgement from the Federal Reserve Board;

---

[196] While this update is outside of the reporting period for this report, it became available before publishing, and so is included.

[197] While this update is outside of the reporting period for this report, it became available before publishing, and so is included.

**October 2, 2012:** Funding Request to the Federal Reserve Board;

**October 18, 2012:** Funding Acknowledgement from the Federal Reserve Board;

**January 7, 2013:** Funding Request to the Federal Reserve Board;

**January 16, 2013:** Funding Acknowledgement from the Federal Reserve Board;

**April 2, 2013:** Funding Request to the Federal Reserve Board;

**April 8, 2013:** Funding Acknowledgement from the Federal Reserve Board;

**October 7, 2013:** Funding Request to the Federal Reserve Board;

**October 15, 2013:** Funding Acknowledgement from the Federal Reserve Board;

**January 7, 2014:** Funding Request to the Federal Reserve Board;

**January 22, 2014:** Funding Acknowledgement from the Federal Reserve Board;

**April 7, 2014:** Funding Request to the Federal Reserve Board;

**April 11, 2014:** Funding Acknowledgement from the Federal Reserve Board;

**July 9, 2014:** Funding Request to the Federal Reserve Board; **and**

**July 28, 2014:** Funding Acknowledgement from the Federal Reserve Board.

# APPENDIX J:

# CFPB organizational chart

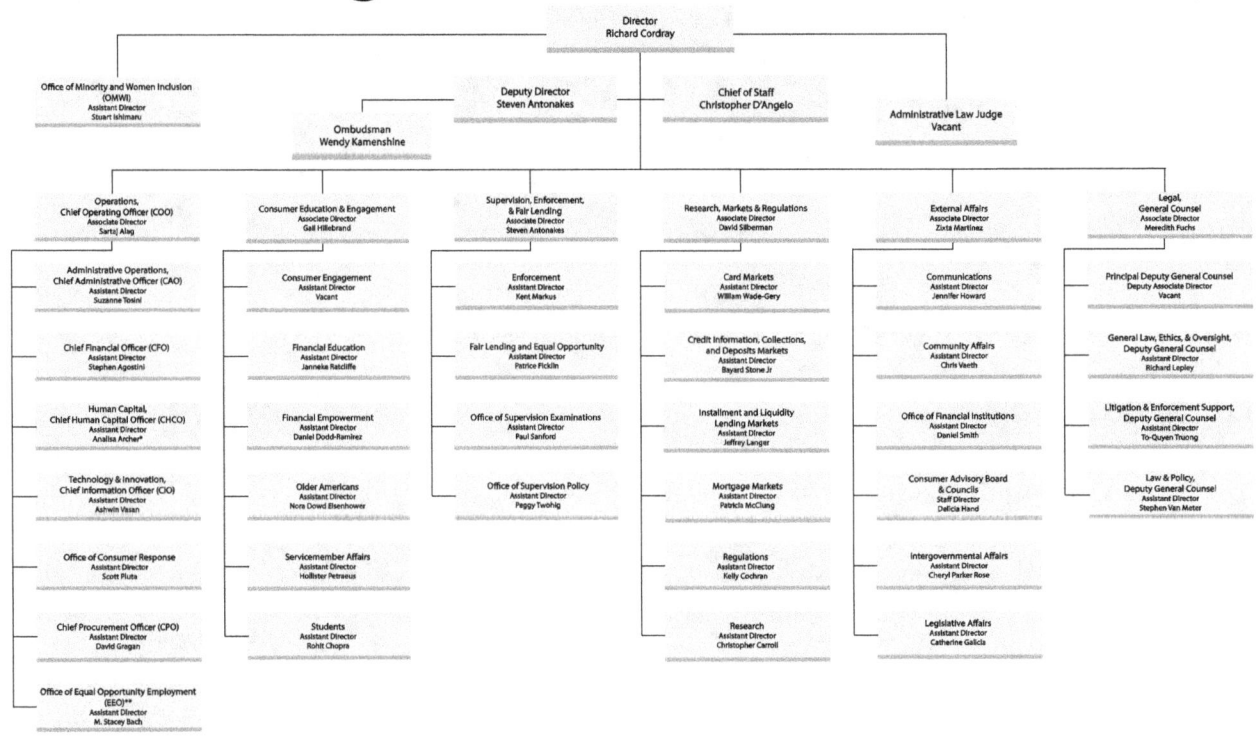

Last updated: November 19, 2014

# APPENDIX K:

# Defined terms

| ACRONYM | DEFINED TERM |
| --- | --- |
| ADSS | American Debt Settlement Solutions |
| ALLY | Ally Financial, Inc. and Ally Bank |
| ANPR | Advance Notice of Proposed Rulemaking |
| ARC | The CFPB's Academic Research Council |
| BUREAU | The Consumer Financial Protection Bureau |
| CAB | The CFPB's Consumer Advisory Board |
| CARD ACT | Credit Card Accountability Responsibility and Disclosure Act of 2009 |
| CBAC | The CFPB's Community Bank Advisory Council |
| CE | The CFPB's Office of Consumer Engagement |
| CEE | The CFPB's Division of Consumer Education and Engagement |
| CFPB | The Consumer Financial Protection Bureau |
| COMMISSION | The U.S. Financial Literacy and Education Commission |
| CONSUMER RESPONSE | The CFPB's Office of Consumer Response |
| CUAC | The CFPB's Credit Union Advisory Council |
| DODD-FRANK ACT | Dodd-Frank Wall Street Reform and Consumer Protection Act |
| DOJ | The U.S. Department of Justice |

| | |
|---|---|
| **DOT** | The U.S. Department of Transportation |
| **ECOA** | Equal Credit Opportunity Act |
| **ECP** | Examiner Commissioning Program |
| **EFTA** | Electronic Fund Transfer Act |
| **EITC** | Earned Income Tax Credit |
| **EMPOWERMENT** | The CFPB's Office of Financial Empowerment |
| **FAIR LENDING** | The CFPB's Office of Fair Lending and Equal Opportunity |
| **FCA** | The U.S. Farm Credit Administration |
| **FDIC** | The U.S. Federal Deposit Insurance Corporation |
| **FEDERAL RESERVE BOARD** | The U.S. Board of Governors of the Federal Reserve System |
| **FFIEC** | The U.S. Federal Financial Institutions Examination Council |
| **FHFA** | The U.S. Federal Housing Finance Agency |
| **FOIA** | Freedom of Information Act |
| **FRB** | The U.S. Board of Governors of the Federal Reserve System |
| **FTC** | The U.S. Federal Trade Commission |
| **FY** | Fiscal Year |
| **GAO** | The U.S. Government Accountability Office |
| **GIPSA** | The Grain Inspection, Packers and Stockyards Administration of the U.S. Department of Agriculture |
| **GLBA** | Gramm-Leach-Bliley Act |
| **HHS** | The U.S. Department of Health and Human Services |
| **HMDA** | Home Mortgage Disclosure Act of 1975 |

| | |
|---|---|
| **HUD** | The U.S. Department of Housing and Urban Development |
| **ICP** | Interim Commissioning Policy |
| **JAG** | Judge Advocate General |
| **LEP** | Limited English Proficiency |
| **MOU** | Memorandum of Understanding |
| **NCRA** | Nationwide Credit Reporting Agencies |
| **NCUA** | The National Credit Union Administration |
| **NLHC** | National Legal Help Center |
| **NSF** | Non-Sufficient Funds |
| **OA** | The CFPB's Office of Older Americans |
| **OAA** | The CFPB's Office of Administrative Adjudication |
| **OCA** | The CFPB's Office of Community Affairs |
| **OCC** | The U.S. Office of the Comptroller of the Currency |
| **ODEP** | The U.S. Department of Labor's Office of Disability Employment Policy |
| **OEEO** | The CFPB's Office of Equal Employment Opportunity |
| **OFE** | The CFPB's Office of Financial Education |
| **OHC** | The CFPB's Office of Human Capital |
| **OIG** | Office of the Inspector General |
| **OJT** | On-the-Job Training |
| **OMWI** | The CFPB's Office of Minority and Women Inclusion |
| **OSA** | The CFPB's Office of Servicemember Affairs |

| | |
|---|---|
| **OTS** | The U.S. Office of Thrift Supervision |
| **PLDS** | Payday Loan Debt Solutions |
| **PROCUREMENT** | The CFPB's Office of Procurement |
| **RESPA** | Real Estate Settlement Procedures Act of 1974 |
| **RMIC** | Republic Mortgage Insurance Company |
| **SCRA** | Servicemembers Civil Relief Act |
| **SEC** | The U.S. Securities and Exchange Commission |
| **SL&D** | Supervision Learning and Development |
| **T&I** | The CFPB's Office of Technology and Innovation |
| **TILA** | Truth in Lending Act |
| **TREASURY** | The U.S. Department of the Treasury |
| **VITA** | Volunteer Income Tax Assistance |